Delegating
Authority

By

Andrew E. Schwartz

Andrew E. Schwartz is president of A.E. Schwartz & Associates, a comprehensive training and consulting organization in Waverley, MA. He is also the training consortium director for the Smaller Business Association of New England and the founder of The Training Consortium, a national network and referral service that matches trainers to organizations. Mr. Schwartz has also taught and lectured at several colleges and universities.

All inquiries should be addressed to:
Barron's Educational Series, Inc.
250 Wireless Boulevard
Hauppauge, New York 11788

Library of Congress Catalog Card Number 91-36616

International Standard Book No. 0-8120-4958-6

Library of Congress Cataloging in Publication Data

Schwartz, Andrew E.
    Delegating authority / by Andrew E. Schwartz.
        p.   cm.
    Includes index.
    ISBN 0-8120-4958-6
    1. Delegation of authority.   I. Title
HD50.S37   1992
658.4'02—dc20

91-36616
CIP

PRINTED IN THE UNITED STATES OF AMERICA

2345   9770   987654321

CONTENTS

DEDICATION

his Book Is Dedicated to: Those special people who have shared and given to me throughout the years—my wife and mother—and in memory of my father.

ACKNOWLEDGMENTS

I am indebted to many organizations, trainers, consultants, writers, and staff who each day apply systems theory to the field of management and have provided many of the insights contained in this publication. I would like to extend specific thanks to several people without whom this project would not have evolved.

A.E. Schwartz & Associates affiliates: To Lynn Feldman, who has taken many concepts and helped make our training program participant materials a written reality; to Douglas Park for his general editing skills; to Lisa Bell for the hours spent typing this document; to Margo Chevers, president of Northeast Leadership Enterprise; and Kerry Stackpole, executive director of The Smaller Business Association of New England, for their contributions and evaluation comments.

Organizations for whom related training programs have been conducted, from which this material has evolved: Sterling Winthrop; Purity Supreme; Solbourne Computers; Weyerhauser Paper; Massachusetts Bay Transportation Authority; Warren (N.J.) Telephone; Warren, Gorham & Lamont; The Boston Company; J.L. Hammett; and many others.

To the staff and editors at Barron's: Thank you!
A.E.S.

INTRODUCTION

B eing a manager isn't easy. Managers have many jobs and duties that require many skills. Managers plan and execute goals and deal with employees by coaching, counseling, and encouraging them, as well as oversee and perform many tasks while making sure they all get done. Successful managers possess excellent interpersonal and communication skills; flexibility and the ability to adapt to a variety of situations; and decisiveness.

A manager's ultimate goal is to maximize the department or work unit productivity and efficiency. As a manager, you need to recognize that you cannot do this by yourself. Nor should you expect to be able to do this by yourself. Remember, you are a person who *manages*. The word manage means to oversee or supervise the operation of something, be it a baseball team, a magazine, or a department within a company. Managers are charged with finding ways to make things run smoothly. One of a manager's best friends in this effort is delegation.

Now you might be thinking, "I don't want to delegate" or "I'm afraid to delegate." You may fear a loss of control or feel that delegation is not worth the effort. Perhaps you're not confident that your staff is competent enough to complete the job. Maybe you don't want to communicate with your staff on a consistent basis. Or perhaps you're thinking, "That stuff doesn't work" or "I don't have the time." Or you may wonder, what if the person you train becomes better at the task than you are? Unpleasant experiences with delegation might also make you wary of trying it again. These are common barriers that unfortunately keep many managers from using delegation to their advantage. Just ask managers who delegate effectively whether or not delegation produces results. Managers who work at and utilize delegation know its helpfulness. One manager attests to delegation's importance in his job: "After I became better at delegating tasks, I found that I was able to spend more time on the important parts of my job, like planning for the department."

The purpose of this book is to help you become an effective delegator and overcome your hesitations about delegation. We will cover the essential skills and techniques of delegation and set the ground rules for you to use delegation in improving the efficiency and productivity of your work unit.

Even if you have had previous exposure to delegation techniques or have had unpleasant experiences with delegation, this book can help you gain proficiency in essential delegation skills and techniques. We're confident you can benefit from this book because of the results our program attendees have seen. Approach this book and its subject matter with a positive, open frame of mind. Get ready to increase your managerial effectiveness by learning how to use delegation to your advantage.

CHAPTER 1

TOWARD A NEW CONCEPTION OF DELEGATION:

Its Benefits and Components

Do not put a sword in a madman's hand.

—English proverb

Chapter Focus: This chapter will show you how to think about delegation in order to improve your delegation skills. The basic components of and issues involved with delegation, including the *why*, *what*, and *who* of delegation, are covered.

Delegation *is* management. To delegate effectively is to manage effectively.

Every month in a sales operation, the end-of-the-month report needs to be compiled to show how much new business has been sold for future months and how much was dropped from the books as a result of the previous month's passing.

All of these figures are broken down into their specific categories that include travel, mileage, tools, lodging, food, office purchases, office supplies, telephone, and out-of-pocket expenses. Then they are further broken down into air carrier, breakfast, lunch, dinner, gratuities, office supplies for both under and over $50.00, and they are also sorted for each sales representative: there are 30 sales reps in my department.

This information is culled from each expense report, entered manually into the monthly backlog sheet by category, and totaled. The totals are then transferred by category to a summary sheet and reconciled.

Do you think that this sounds like a lot of work? It certainly is! It takes a full day to compile these figures.

As sales manager for a large telecommunications department, this report was one of my responsibilities each month. I, however, wanting to be an efficient manager, would delegate this task to a different salesperson each month and spotcheck that work. I developed an instruction guide to assist them and verbally communicated each month with the designated sales representative.

We experienced the usual problems doing it in this way, but nothing that I considered insurmountable—until I hired a new employee to take over all the paperwork. She was bright, organized, and I never had a doubt of her ability to handle this complex task.

At the end of the month I gave her the assignment of doing the month-end report. I explained its purpose, how to do it, showed her by example, and asked if she had any questions. She assured me that she was all set.

I went about my business. Toward the end of the day, I asked her how it was going. She told me it was taking much longer than she anticipated. She asked if she could finish it the next day.

I told her that my first time tackling it had been a challenge, too.

Well, the next day she toiled over it again, but at the end of the day, the information would not reconcile. It was not even close. I offered my help. She refused it, saying that she was going to lick the problem herself.

The following day, she again pursued the task, but found that she was in worse trouble than the previous day. I kept asking her if she wanted help.

"No, I can do this myself," was her reply. By the end of the day, her frustration level was so high that she marched into my office with the stack of paperwork and said, "I can't do this, I need your help. Could you do this for me?"

Have you ever played detective uncovering someone else's accounting mistakes? It is one of the greatest and most frustrating challenges I have ever encountered.

Three days later, I finally had untangled the web of figures and found the reconciled numbers to present to upper management. They were quite upset that the report had taken so long.

It took six days to do a task that normally took one!

My reaction? Never again did I delegate that task. I could not take the chance of this happening again and did not feel comfortable giving it back to the sales representatives who were glad to have it taken off their list of duties.

What happened after I stopped delegating the task?

My time, which was much more valuable than that of anyone on my staff, was taken up one day each month on a task that could have been done by someone else.

Now you're probably saying, "That makes sense, given your experience." But take a look at my experience. Only once did I experience a problem; the rest of the time the sales staff performed superbly. My reaction was unwarranted.

I later found out that the other members of the sales staff felt I was not trusting them by no longer delegating tasks. They hadn't made mistakes. They had always performed well. Now they believed that I was withholding information from them. Additionally, I was not able to give them as much time as in the past.

You see, I never realized that delegation not only lessened my work load, but it was also an excellent method of building the knowledge and responsibility level within my sales force. While compiling the report, the sales people were able to see how the various expenses affected the organization and the bottom line. They had become more cost-conscious and helpful in recommendations to save money. They had been exposed to the seasonal changes and recognized potential problems in the different categories.

Because of my unwillingness to work with one employee more closely, I had taken away an opportunity for the sales representatives to grow in their positions and toward management. I also hurt morale, cost the organization money, created more pressure for myself, took time away from more potentially productive areas, and failed to provide a good role model.

Do you often see these symptoms of poor delegation in your workplace?

- *The "I-thought-it-was-done" syndrome.* The assignment you thought had been completed last week unexpectedly shows up incomplete. Good delegation practices inform people about schedules, expectations, and status situations.

- *Piles of work.* Everyone is always playing catch-up. You have overnight or weekend homework. *The backload continues to build up.* Crisis situations constantly arise as deadlines approach. These problems stem from poor delegation practices. Rid yourself of these headaches!

- *The almost-successful project.* This project could have been a boom, but instead it was a bust because it was conceived at only one level. Ideas from various levels would have given the foresight needed for the plan to achieve its full potential.

- *The overloaded manager.* This manager is *always* struggling to complete several jobs at the same time. The workflow never stops. Are this manager's delegation practices crying for reform? A checkup sure wouldn't hurt.

- *Unenthusiastic employees.* Employees are disappointed and unhappy about the manager's perceived lack of confidence in their capabilities. Challenge your employees and help them to develop by using delegation effectively.

CLASSIC WARNING SIGNS

Read the following situation, and consider whether any of the problems mentioned have arisen during your attempts to delegate.

> You have just given an employee the task of checking facts on a research project. You tell him, "I don't have time for this. Check this over and give it back to me when you're done." Being busy, you quickly walk away, expecting the job to be completed in three weeks.
>
> The employee is left in a quandary because of the vague instructions. He is wondering, "Exactly what am I supposed to do? What is the deadline on this project?" and concludes, "Well, I have too many other assignments to complete, so I'll just wait until the boss comes back to talk to me about it."
>
> Three weeks pass by and you say to the employee, "I'd like to see the report that I gave you three weeks ago." He responds, "You never told me exactly what to do with it or when it was due."
>
> You quickly realize the errors you made when delegating the task. You were overloaded, so you hastily decided to dump the work onto someone else. However, you didn't tell the employee what you expected, what was to be done, or the time frame for the project. You also should have checked up on his progress and communicated with him during the

project. What can you do to prevent these problems in the future?

If you see these classic warning signs of poor delegation in your department or organization, this book is for you. Instead of suffering from these problems, use the techniques in this book to make delegation work for you.

TRADITIONAL CONCEPTIONS OF DELEGATION

Delegation is a powerful tool that can help managers improve the performance of their work unit. Unfortunately, traditional conceptions of delegation often make this tool underutilized and misunderstood. Notions of delegation such as "abdicating responsibility for a task," "letting someone else do the dirty work," and "giving a job to someone who can't do it well" shroud delegation in negative connotations that inhibit managers from tapping delegation's full potential.

These conceptions, together with other obstacles, hinder the effective use of delegation by many managers. Among these attitudes are:

- *Distrust of employees.* "My staff is not capable of handling that job."
- *Reluctance to share power.* "Things get all confused when more than one person has power on a project."
- *Misunderstanding of delegation.* "Delegation is too time-consuming."
- *Fear of delegation.* "Delegation is a high-risk proposition."
- *Overly detail-oriented.* "I want to be involved in the process every step of the way."
- *My way only.* "It has to be done this way or no way at all."
- *Perfectionism.* "It won't be done right if it is done by my employees."

- *Playing it safe.* "If I delegate, I will have to do things that I'm less accustomed to."

Stop! Do you hold any of these ideas about delegation? If you do, overhauling your thinking about delegation will make you a more effective manager. In this book, we will introduce a new conception of delegation that will broaden your thinking about the topic and also enable you to take advantage of an essential management skill.

Indeed, delegation *is* management. Your job as a manager is to make sure your department operates smoothly under your direction. That means guiding the department by using the available resources—including your staff—optimally. To delegate effectively, then, is to manage effectively.

A PROPOSED DEFINITION OF DELEGATION

Our definition of delegation begins with a broad, general framework about the art and science of delegation. Delegation can occur in any direction within an organization, from a manager to a staff member (downward), from a manager to another manager (laterally), and from a staff member to a manager (upward). Traditional conceptions of delegation often limit it to a downward transfer of a task or project, yet thinking of delegation as downward, lateral, or upward will enhance its benefits to you and your organization.

Delegation is the entrusting of a specific task or project by one individual to another. You are transferring a particular task or project that you either assign to an employee or normally perform.

Delegation is usually a temporary procedure, although it is possible for a delegated task to evolve into a permanent duty for an employee. Three aspects of delegation—responsibility, authority, and accountability—deserve further clarification.

Responsibility. Contrary to what many managers believe, the *delegator* retains ultimate responsibility for the successful completion of a task. You have final control over the situation, supervising it as you see fit. The delegatee, however, is responsible for meeting specific, intermediate goals of the project.

Authority. Although experts disagree on whether authority can be delegated, it can be transferred for the delegated project within a limited context. Sufficient authority should be transferred to the delegatees to enable them to command the resources necessary to assure that results meet the delegator's objectives and schedule, even if this means expanding the delegatees' authority during the given task.

Accountability. Delegatees should be held accountable for the established goals and must understand how their performance will be judged.

Progress reports and evaluations are useful here. Employees should understand that their judgments, methods, and mistakes will be evaluated, and that they can and will be replaced if their performance is unsatisfactory.

Within these guidelines, you should encourage creativity, cleverness, and originality when you delegate. Give staff the freedom to be innovative in problem-solving, even if their methods are not the same as yours. Allow them to make their own mistakes, learn from them, and then try again. The delegation should be a learning experience for the delegatees, so let them learn a lesson from it.

Remembering the "Two T's," trust and time, will greatly aid in accomplishing effective delegation.

- *Trust.* While some employees may truly lack the skills, experience, or training to complete a task, you need to trust your employees. When deficiencies exist, restructure jobs, train, or reassign employees. Often, however, you may simply need to have a little more faith in your employees. Showing your staff that you trust them will give them self-confidence. Give them the free rein they need in order to do what you asked them to do.

- *Time.* Many managers begin the delegation process well, but fizzle out as the process unfolds. Take time to provide miniappraisals and feedback for the delegatee. While delegation may require an initial time investment, this will more than pay itself off in the long run.

Delegation is not a one-step action, but rather an ongoing process with many components. Trust and time therefore epitomize our new conception of delegation that envisions the process as a relationship between two or more people. As in any relationship, you must invest time and show trust for the delegation to be successful.

BENEFITS OF EFFECTIVE DELEGATION

Effective delegation can reap many benefits for organizations, employees, and managers.

Organizational Reasons to Delegate

- *To save money for the organization.* Calculate what an hour of your time costs your organization and then compare it to that of your employees. Every task you delegate to one of them represents a substantial cost savings.

- *To ensure that work is done by the right person.* No managers, regardless of their competence, can adequately perform each departmental function as well as the person who does it on a daily basis. Many have not worked their way up through the company, and those who have are unlikely to have handled all aspects of a process. Additionally, they would hardly have been promoted to a managerial position without the organization's belief that their talents could best be used there. Effective delegation ensures that each task be performed at the lowest appropriate level.

- *To have better trained, more capable employees.* Delegation can help employees develop skills, motivation, and self-confidence, qualities that are beneficial to any organization. Furthermore, delegation assignments can groom employees for promotion, thereby providing the organization with more desirable employees. Any organization attempts to secure the most qualified employees possible, and effective delegation can help attain that goal.

- *To build teamwork, cohesion, and spirit.* Employees who receive delegation assignments feel better about themselves, their jobs, and their managers. As managers and employees develop relationships during delegation projects, teamwork and cohesion are cultivated. All organizations strive to achieve teamwork, cohesion, and spirit; delegation gets you closer to these goals.

- *To increase productivity and efficiency.* Freeing managers for tasks only they can perform and optimizing the use of human resources increase overall productivity and efficiency. Also, by reducing stress for managers and providing challenges for employees, productivity and efficiency are promoted.

Employee-Related Reasons to Delegate

- *To increase motivation, confidence, and personal as well as professional growth.* On-the-job training challenges employees to evaluate risks, make decisions, and handle conflicts, while preparing them for promotion. Effective delegation also heightens interest in the company and instills pride by demonstrating the manager's faith in employees' abilities.

- *To develop skills.* Effective delegation will challenge and enhance employees' abilities in making decisions and solving problems, as well as working with other people on projects.

- *To give a sense of achievement.* Employees will feel good about their jobs knowing that they have completed concrete tasks and achieved predetermined goals. In turn, they will be more enthusiastic about their work.

Managerial Reasons to Delegate

- *To effectively maximize time.* Delegation frees management from routine and repetitive functions. Managers are most cost-effective when directing their energies to those top-level duties for which they were hired and are being paid—planning, setting objectives, developing policies, and measuring results. Delegation multiplies your productivity.

- *To reduce stress.* Work overload can cause stress for a manager, but effective delegation can lighten the psychological burden of routine and noncrucial tasks that can induce stress.

Clearly, effective delegation can be advantageous to an organization as well as its employees and managers. These advantages warrant a closer look at the delegation process.

STARTING THE PROCESS

Deciding What to Delegate

You might now be saying, "Well, now that I know what delegation is and what it's good for, how do I do it?"

First, clarify for yourself the parameters of the delegation by considering and answering the following questions:

What is the purpose of the delegation? To decrease my workload, develop an employee, or complete a blueprint early? One delegation project may achieve several purposes.

Should I delegate this task? Knowing the purpose of the assignment helps in determining whether or not to delegate a task. This check serves to ensure that the task is better done by someone other than yourself.

What exactly do I want done? Specify the scope of the assignment.

Thinking along these lines will help you explain an assignment more easily to the delegatee. Give as much detail as necessary.

Begin the delegation relationship by choosing the tasks that you will delegate. Experience dictates that some jobs can be delegated, while others cannot. You can divide your workload into three categories: (1) tasks you can delegate, (2) delegation during crises, and (3) tasks you should not delegate.

1. Tasks you should delegate. The following tasks can usually be delegated:

Routine Jobs

Fact-gathering—If the job is time-consuming (e.g., requires library research), it may make sense to delegate the job to a detail-oriented employee.

Departmental routines—Every department has routine procedures, such as filling out time cards and answering questions from other parts of the organization. Such responsibilities can generally be delegated to capable employees.

Clerical assignments—Delegate tasks such as completing simple forms, purchase orders, and the like. Do not delegate sensitive financial assignments that require your knowledge or authorization.

Thinking/Judgment Jobs

Problem-solving—When the item is not of vital importance, you may want to consider the

13

option of allowing one or more employees to try their hands at it.

Reports—When employees are capable or can easily be briefed, let them write the report.

Planning—Planning should seldom be delegated since it is a responsibility unique to your position. But a planning assignment can challenge particularly capable employees.

Supervision—A project team usually requires a group leader. This person should work closely with you and possess limited authority.

Screening resumes—This can be a difficult and delicate job. The delegatee should understand the judging criteria for desirable traits, immediate rejection, and similar factors.

People/Relational Jobs

Meetings—Pick a mature and well-qualified employee who can stay within the boundaries of the assigned role, but be sure to specify limits to his/her participation.

Relations with other departments—Since cooperation and diplomacy are important in interdepartmental relationships, avoid delegating this duty to conflict-prone employees. You should establish a liaison with the heads of other departments to minimize the likelihood of miscommunication.

Training—This task is commonly but often mistakenly delegated. Avoid the usual mistakes such as giving a training role to a poor teacher (be sure that you check that individual's training practices to determine this) or choosing employees who may not put their full efforts into the training. Check employees' progress during training.

2. Delegation during crises. If you have to leave the workplace due to an emergency, delegation may become necessary to keep the department operating. In these situations, *how* you delegate is as important as *what* you delegate. During crises, you should consider exercising the following options:

Leave instructions—Although you may be in a hurry, a few quick words may not yield a satisfactory performance. Take the time to give careful instructions.

Postpone—Wait until you return to complete as many tasks as possible.

Designate a substitute—Ask a fellow executive or your boss to act as a source of guidance for employees who may become confused or unable to perform in your absence. Be sure to give your substitute a quick summary of crucial information.

3. Tasks you should not delegate. Some activities are better left undelegated. You may need to delay working on them until you can personally tend to them. Tasks falling into this category include:

Discipline—The power to discipline individuals is the foundation of executive authority. This power should not be transferred to anyone.

Tasks for which no employee is qualified—An executive says to an employee, "I've been wondering whether we should consider converting some of our paper files to computer files. Will you study the possibilities of a computer database? Investigate cost and feasibility, and report back on whether you think it's a good idea for the department."

Unless the manager is thoroughly familiar with the capabilities of the delegatee, and thus knows that the employee can respond to such vague instructions, this executive is not delegating effectively. The matter under question involves topics that many employees are not likely to know about. Without detailed information, a realistic assessment cannot be made. In this case, even an experienced executive might have difficulty assessing the situation without an expert opinion.

The complex situation—Don't expect an employee to deal with a situation that befuddles you or for which you have no ready solution. For example, handling a delicate negotiation with a customer or addressing a situation crucial to your career are matters that undoubtedly require your personal attention, no matter how capable the employee. These tasks cannot be delegated.

Maintaining morale—Your leadership directly fosters the attitudes of your work group—make sure those attitudes are positive. You may call upon others to help with activities that boost morale, but the final responsibility for morale, as well as deciding what level of group morale is acceptable, is yours.

Certain other tasks that should never be delegated include: work that involves confidential information; "crash programs" that usually demand the experience and expertise of management; and tasks involving supervisor-staff relations such as employee evaluations, compensation, and counseling.

Work that is to be delegated should follow these five general guidelines:

1. It can be handled to completion with appropriate follow-through without undue difficulty.
2. All information necessary for decision making is also available for the later stages of the assignment.

3. The work involves operational detail rather than planning or organization.

4. The task does not require skills unique to the manager or position.

5. Essentially, an individual other than the manager has (or can have) direct control over the task.

Remember, you can discuss a task or situation without delegating it. Employees may have the objectivity and maturity to help you put a difficult situation into perspective. Many executives have found it helpful to ask the opinions of their employees at all levels on crucial matters in broadening their perspective. But they are seeking experience and opinions, not avenues for delegation.

Delegating a Situation Rather Than a Task

The idea of delegating a situation increases the scope of the delegation assignment. Delegating a situation is delegating a miniproject or a series of related tasks that together constitute a situation. If you have employees who are capable of handling broad responsibility, you should consider this option.

Delegating situations allows you to pass on a larger segment of your workload and to clear the way for higher-priority items. Consider the following points before utilizing this technique:

- *Put the situation in context.* You may need to supply the history and background of the situation to the delegatee. Describe how the situation affects the organization as a whole.

- *Have a good reason.* Because it can be tempting to overuse this approach, be sure you need to delegate a situation as opposed to a task. One advantage to delegating a situation is that it brings a new perspective to a problem that may have become too complicated to be handled piecemeal. Skilled delegatees like

17

receiving a situation because they have the opportunity to test and improve themselves in managerial action.

- *Ask for a complete briefing.* It is advisable to have your delegatee submit a detailed written or verbal report to make sure that all the major parts have been covered.

- *Using the guidelines and tips provided, you should divide all of your current tasks into three categories*: (1) work that only you, the manager, can perform; (2) work that can be delegated immediately; and (3) work that can be delegated as soon as an employee can be trained to handle it.

Delegating the Whole Task

Whenever possible, you should delegate a whole task to one person rather than divide it among several individuals. There may, however, be occasions in which work must be divided among several individuals, as with highly technical or large tasks. Should this be the case, the rule is to *delegate the maximum amount of work to the lowest possible level.*

For example, let's say a report that must be completed in two days requires a final accuracy check of the quarter's sales figures. This is a detail-oriented job that one person probably could not complete alone. In this situation, you would want to give as much of the job as possible to employees who would not have more important duties to fulfill. You could split the job among one or two employees, giving each the figures for a specific division. Research assistants might be a good choice for this delegation. You would not want to create a "brain drain" by giving the job to other managers or to office professionals.

Delegating a whole task increases an employee's initiative, encourages greater attention to detail, and gives a manager greater control over results. Furthermore, it minimizes confusion and eliminates unnecessary and inefficient coordination of efforts among two or more employees. All of these factors lead to more successful results.

Delegating the whole task, however, does not mean dumping an assignment on an employee without specific preparation, training, and coaching. This is especially true for those new to the job or those who have not previously been assigned responsibility or authority. Delegation should be a gradual process, allowing staffers to assume responsibility and authority at a comfortable pace. Creating an amicable environment can go a long way towards motivating employees to perform up to their potential.

After a task has been delegated to a staff member, the manager must not take it back, make changes in the assignment, or redelegate it. Such actions greatly frustrate employees. In fact, they may lose their motivation and interest in the project, and entertain doubts as to whether they will ever be allowed to complete it.

If the delegatee should reach an impasse and turn to the manager for answers, the manager should immediately put the ball back in the employee's court and ask, "What do you recommend?" This forces the employee to come up with a solution and provides the manager with a means of evaluating the employee's thinking and judgment process. Taking back incomplete work, for whatever reason, fosters dependence and indicates a failed delegation.

Selecting the Right Person

Having decided what to delegate, the next decision you must make is to whom the task will be delegated. The right person to delegate to is not always the most skillful or experienced. Your selection will depend on the situation, nature of the job, and purposes of the delegation. Selecting the right employee to do the work is an evaluative process, and you must be able to identify individuals both capable and willing to handle responsibility.

One variable influencing your choice is the demands of the situation. Is it necessary that the job be done in the shortest possible time? Is accuracy absolutely essential? You must examine all your options and demands before making a choice.

Carefully review past assumptions about personnel. Some employees' capabilities may have been overestimated, others underestimated. A personnel survey or personal interviews are excellent ways to reassess your staff. Both can (1) determine the additional duties that can now be adequately handled by each person and (2) indicate the goals and direction toward which each employee aspires. These methods provide you with insight into employee interests and aspirations, and at the same time, they will also pinpoint those presently qualified for delegation.

You should also consider which employees have made independent decisions within the parameters of their positions and authority, and whether these decisions were "right," even though they may not necessarily have been in accordance with past management decisions. Employees are certainly ready for more responsibility and authority when they have shown the ability to make decisions that are both innovative and fruitful.

After the evaluation process is completed, you should be able to separate those employees to whom delegation can be made with a high chance of success from those who are unsuited for delegation. Show patience. Employees' ability to handle added responsibility and authority comes in stages.

Here are five simple rules to guide your selection of employees for delegation assignments:

1. *The employee must be available for the assignment.* If necessary, choose the individual whose work can be most easily interrupted.

2. *Match the skills of your employees to the demands of the task.* If speed is of the utmost importance, choose a fast worker. If speed is critical, and you have picked the person who generally performs fastest, be sure that you double-check the work either in progress or upon completion to make sure that you haven't sacrificed quality for speed.

3. *Try to spread your delegations among as many of your employees as possible.* It is generally unwise to limit your delegations to one or two employees. This action may be viewed as favoritism, and you lose the training advantages that delegation can bring to a work group. By limiting delegation, you may lose the stimulation and cooperation that comes when everyone in the group feels that you trust them enough to give them a chance to assist you with tasks outside their own immediate responsibility.

4. *Avoid delegating tasks to employees during the first three months of their tenure.* Give new employees time to settle into their jobs, learn the ropes, and feel comfortable with their assigned responsibilities before adding new ones.

5. *Don't overlook the possibility of assigning the task to two or more people.* Some tasks will need two or more people. When three or more people have been delegated a task, you may need to assign a group leader. Also, if it is desirable to delegate to someone other than your direct employee, discuss the assignment with the individual's immediate supervisor. It may be desirable for the employee's supervisor to assign the task. If you are going to make the assignment, do so with the supervisor present.

When an Employee Offers to Take a Delegation Assignment

An employee may occasionally ask for an assignment that is a delegation of your work rather than a task having to do with a regular job. Consider the following example:

Secretary Ann Dent approaches her boss and says, "Mr. Lee, I heard you talking to the maintenance director about getting new carpeting and wallpaper. I got the impression that you really don't want to deal with it. I studied some interior design, and I love the idea of choosing colors and styles. Would you consider letting me help you with the project?"

Most managers would like to be in Mr. Lee's position. He will be relieved of a task he considers bothersome while also having his secretary benefit from a new and challenging assignment. He may even end up with a design plan that is better than the one he would have had without Ann Dent's help.

Although employees technically can't "volunteer" for a delegation assignment, they can ask for permission to handle it. Such requests usually indicate enthusiastic and aspiring employees who are looking to enrich their jobs.

Unless there is a valid reason for rejecting the offer—for example, if the assignment requires special training or other employees are as qualified and deserving as the employee who approaches you—it is in your best interest to make the delegation. In most cases, an employee who wants more responsibility is a desirable employee.

The self-imposed test will also show whether or not the employee has the qualities needed to perform the job satisfactorily, which is useful for you to know in the future.

THE COMPONENTS OF DELEGATION

Having discussed the *what* and *to whom* of delegation, we can move on to the actual process. Delegation can be thought of as a process that consists of five basic components—goal-setting, communication, supervision, motivation, and evaluation. We will briefly discuss these components to set the direction for the rest of the book.

Goal-setting. You must work with the delegatee to determine the expectations and goals that you can realistically set. Specify concrete, measurable goals and objectives that can be evaluated. Unclear, vague goals increase the likelihood of failure. Most importantly, put the goals in writing so that there can be no misunderstanding. You clarify what you want in your important personal relationships—do the same in your delegation relationships.

You'll find tips in Chapter 2 on how to use goal-setting in delegation.

Communication. Communication is the foundation of proper delegation. Give your staff feedback during the delegation process. Keep in mind that delegation involves two-way communication between the delegator and delegatee. In your delegation activities, learn and practice the principles of two-way communication that will be outlined in Chapter 3.

Motivation. Difficult or uninteresting delegated tasks sometimes require that you take measures to motivate the delegatee to achieve predetermined goals. The process of motivating employees must take into account special considerations unique to the delegation project. You should also learn how delegation can motivate. Motivation is an important part of delegations, and Chapter 4 will show you the way.

Supervision. Although delegation is designed to lighten your load, you must still supervise the delegatee during the process. Supervising a delegation, however, is a delicate and tricky endeavor. Normal supervision procedures must be modified to meet the special circumstances of a delegation project.

A useful way to conceive of the supervisor/employee relationship during delegation projects is introduced in Chapter 5.

Evaluation. Delegation is not a quick, one-step process; progress reports and evaluations are integral parts. You must review the extent to which goals were met, the operation of the process, and how the process could be improved. Use evaluations to set goals, communicate, supervise, and motivate. Evaluations are another means by which to strengthen your relationship with the delegatee, and you will learn how to conduct them in Chapter 6.

In summary, delegation is the entrusting of a specific task or project by one person to another. Delegation is a relationship between two people. It requires time and trust to work well. As in any organizational relationship, delegation requires goal-setting, communication, supervision, motivation, and evaluation. Our conception of delegation is much more complex and effective than the traditional ideas that perceive it as a pass-the-buck measure. This book shows you how to delegate effectively.

CHAPTER 2

GOAL-SETTING:

The What, When, and How-to

If you do not know where you are going, you will probably wind up somewhere else.

—Dr. Laurence J. Peter

C*hapter Focus*: This chapter will discuss the importance of goal-setting; how to begin the goal-setting process; and how to delineate, communicate, and implement goals in delegating.

The belief that setting goals for a delegation project is unnecessary is linked to a common fallacy—the notion that delegation is a simple process requiring minimal attention.

Imagine trying to run a race without a finish line. It doesn't make much sense. There is no way to determine when you have finished or how to pace yourself. Since there is no way for you to tell how well you are doing, you will probably drop out of the race. Goals provide the motivating force that make activities productive. Contrary to popular belief, goal-setting is not a complicated process. It merely requires that management and staff communicate.

Many employees, however, are doomed to perform delegation projects unsatisfactorily because they're not sure where the finish line is. Failed assignments can often be turned into successes by successfully using the widely misunderstood and underutilized managerial tool of goal-setting. Unfortunately, the process of goal-setting is often either improperly implemented or completely ignored.

THE WHAT, WHEN, AND HOW OF GOAL-SETTING

The *what*, *when*, and *how* questions define the goal-setting process. Answering these four questions will greatly aid in goal attainment.

1. *What* is to be done? Spell out the goal for the employee. Nothing can be more demotivating than uncertainty about what to do. An employee's motivation level is directly linked to accomplishing stated tasks; when a sense of accomplishment is missing, job satisfaction will usually decline.

2. *When* is it to be completed? While everyone usually agrees that a supervisor must be as flexible as possible in goal-setting, it is quite easy to establish a vague or unrealistic time frame for completion. Time frames should be realistic and definite, yet flexible. For example, many times within the work environment, situations will arise that could not have been anticipated when the goal was actually set.

3. *How* will the goal be reached? Always try to recognize the resources required for goal achievement. In some cases, no outside assistance is required. In other situations, a great deal of coaching and training is necessary. Furthermore, the employee's other priorities must be considered to avoid possible conflicts later on. Don't fall into the trap of having an employee succeed on one particular goal and thereby fail on several others. As with other managerial techniques, it is well worth the effort to plan before committing time and resources to a delegation.

4. *How* will success be measured? This question focuses on whether the goal or objective to be assigned is easily measurable in terms of quantity or whether there are also qualitative factors involved. Just as important, it also addresses the evaluation criteria, which can be easily overlooked.

When an organization and its individual members pull together to link their goals, overall success is the result. Personal goals facilitate performance by helping to focus and direct an individual's energy and resources, which creates a sense of accomplishment that gives direction in reaching a goal. Demonstrate how the employee's and the delegation's goals are linked. Combining departmental and personal goals, especially specific and challenging ones, produces high performance and effort levels.

Goal-setting is particularly important to the delegation process. Setting concrete, measurable, attainable goals is the basis for authority, accountability, and responsibility. Without clear goals, it is unreasonable, useless, and, in fact, impossible to transfer these things to a delegatee. Goals establish boundaries around the delegation project and improve its chances of success. A delegation project without goals associated with it cannot be described clearly to an employee before the work is begun, nor evaluated properly afterwards.

GOAL-SETTING AND DELEGATION

Goal-setting can make the delegation process move more smoothly in three ways:

1. *It narrows the manager-employee gap.* Misunderstandings, miscommunication, and noncommunication between management and employees often occur regarding the goals of a delegation project. A supervisor can bridge the gap by setting reasonable goals with each employee. After all, the employees actually perform the required work, and a lack of communication can leave them feeling frustrated and confused about what has been delegated to them.

2. *It provides a realistic assessment of expectations.* The goal-setting process provides a "reality check" of a manager's expectations for a delegation. This process also tests a manager's ability to be specific and detailed with employees. Merely conveying a general idea of goals to employees will not automatically ensure that the goals will be met. Goals must be carefully explained and thoroughly understood.

3. *It ensures the goal's achievement.* Effective goal-setting provides a platform for the continuous coaching process that necessarily follows it. Using a clear and measurable goal as a starting point greatly facilitates the techniques of coaching. If a supervisor monitors progress, any errors that may endanger or stall the goal's completion can be caught early. It is also far easier for a supervisor to coach well when both the employee and the supervisor know in advance the expected performance level.

Successful goal-setting does not always come easily, and a supervisor must recognize that goal-setting can sometimes be extremely difficult. The bright side of the picture, however, is that once everyone recognizes that goal-setting is the first step toward successful performance, the process is well on its way.

HOW TO SET GOALS

Goal-setting can be divided into five basic steps: (1) Specifying the task, (2) Describing and communicating goals, (3) Determining performance criteria, (4) Constructing an action plan, and (5) Introducing and implementing the goal.

STEP 1. Specifying the Task

Traditionally, one of the biggest complaints employees have about the delegation process is that no goal or objective was ever specified. Delineate in detail what is to be done, for yourself. You must know the goals before you can communicate them to the delegatee. Identify the primary objective, and then specify the four to six most important parts of the primary objective, as in the following example.

Primary objective: Gather employee opinions on proposed vacation-time policy changes.

Components

- distribute surveys
- schedule interviews with employees
- compile data and perform statistical analysis
- present findings in report to supervisor with conclusions
- work with others if necessary

STEP 2. Describing and Communicating Goals

Follow certain guidelines as you write the goals and objectives of the delegation project. The presentation of the delegation's goals significantly influences the likelihood of successful goal attainment.

Quantify goals. Goals should be stated in quantifiable terms. Although certain tasks are difficult to measure this way, you should try to quantify goals as much as possible. This can be especially important in giving the delegatee a clear task to complete.

For example, a delegation might have the general goal of "reducing the amount of paper in the office." The goal cannot be measured as described, making it difficult for the delegatee to meet the manager's expectations. Solve the problem by quantifying the goal in a realistic, feasible fashion that will also ensure successful completion of the task. In this case, you might change the goal to "reduce number of file cabinets by 25 percent and convert two file cabinets to computer storage" (assuming that the delegatee is computer-literate).

Make goals clear and easily understandable. Consider the following objective: "To facilitate mail delivery for international employees in the department." Most people would probably ask the following questions about the goal:

- What does "facilitate" mean? How will we know when the goal is met?

- What does "mail delivery" mean? Does this refer to incoming or outgoing mail?

- What does "international" mean? Does this mean employees from a country other than America, employees who deal with customers from different countries, or what?

Such ambiguous language causes confusion and hinders the successful achievement of an otherwise attainable goal. A clear goal, on the other hand, can help a delegatee to complete a task. For example, the above goal could be reworded as follows: "The goal is making sure that mail arriving from international destinations arrives at the sales associates' mailbox within one day of receipt in the mailroom, and that it leaves the building within a day of leaving the associates' desks. Sales associates whose client base consists of at least 50 percent international customers are affected. The goal is to be accomplished within three months."

Make goals challenging. What happens when goals are easily attained? At first glance, this would appear to be a comfortable position for any employee! After all, if a goal is easily met, then goal accomplishment is assured with little effort. Is this an ideal situation?

Consider this example: Employees are delegated simple tasks such as making follow-up calls or writing letters. While the employees appreciate these diversifying activities, they want to stretch their capacities by being given more challenging tasks. The employees are getting restless, bored, discontented, and unmotivated because the goals of the delegations can be easily achieved. Employees need to be challenged by goals that will inspire more thinking and harder work.

Make goals realistic. On the other hand, while goals should be challenging, they should also reflect a realistic estimate of the time and effort needed to accomplish them. Obviously, there will always be a fine line plus several shades of gray, between challenging and realistic, possible and impossible. Moreover, given two employees of equal talent and ability, a particular goal might be viewed as entirely possible by one and utterly impossible by the other!

The astute supervisor thoroughly knows the capabilities of each employee and carefully sets goals within each employee's comfort zone—that is, a reachable goal, provided that additional effort is directed towards its ultimate achievement. That target is not always easy for the first-line supervisor to hit precisely, but it is certainly worth aiming for.

Do not make the assignment too challenging, though. Make sure the delegatees are able to complete the task at their current skill and experience levels.

Word goals affirmatively. Use positive, active words rather than negative, defensive ones. Wording goals affirmatively can have a positive psychological impact upon the person for whom the goal is intended. Affirmative words encourage forward, progressive action, not merely fighting to prevent something from happening. For example, use "Do…" instead of "Don't…."

STEP 3. Determining Performance Criteria

You need to develop the standards of performance, along with the yardsticks for measuring that performance, that will enable you and the delegatee to monitor performance. The two questions to be addressed are (1) What criteria will be used to measure results? and (2) What is the minimum level of performance expected of the delegatee? Remember, the standards should be quantifiable, just like the goals.

STEP 4. Constructing an Action Plan

Many goal- and objective-setting efforts break down because of insufficient attention to this step. Setting goals and objectives is useless without concrete plans to achieve them.

In addition, individuals sometimes achieve their objectives but do so in the wrong way. This happens when the individual focuses only on results rather than the methods needed to reach them. Obviously, both the results and the approaches a person uses to get those results are important.

Encourage the delegatee to spend time answering these questions:

- What actions will I take to achieve the desired results?
- What means will I use?

Remember to give the employee time to think about these issues in order to achieve a sense of self-confidence and the feeling of contributing to the process.

You do not need to focus on lengthy and detailed plans for all goals and objectives. Instead, you and the employee should thoroughly discuss the goals themselves and how the delegatee will achieve them. A discussion with your employee will allow you to share whatever knowledge and experience you may have that can be of help.

The goal here is mutual understanding. Time spent talking about the delegatee's plans to accomplish the goals and objectives will prevent unpleasant surprises later.

Have the employee think about these areas to help in developing an action plan:

- *Time frame.* What is the schedule going to be? How will progress be measured and monitored?

- *Personnel.* Who will be involved? Who will do what? Do those involved have the knowledge and skill to handle the job? What personnel changes need to be made?

- *Finances.* How will cash, checks, or purchase orders be handled? What factors might cause cost overruns?

- *Other.* What factors favor success? What factors are likely to work against success? What can I do to change the inhibiting factors? What future changes would interfere with success? How can I anticipate these possible changes?

Suppose you have given your employee the task of moving files into storage. You say to the employee, "Let's think about how we can best do this. This project will take about one month. How do you think we should schedule the moving? Who should do this? Should we use outside people or our own people? Also think about the distraction this might cause or adjustments we might have to make. We'll discuss your ideas in two days, and I'll give my own ideas as well."

In this way, you give the employee an opportunity to contribute and work with you in constructing an action plan.

STEP 5. Introducing and Implementing the Goal

Goals must be set in a proper climate. A positive climate (where the employee does not feel threatened and is encouraged to ask for clarification) provides the possibility of two-way feedback.

For example, introduce a delegation in a quiet, private setting, such as an office. This type of environment ensures that a transmitted goal or objective will be absolutely clear to the delegatee.

Here is an example of how *not* to introduce a goal:

You and the employee are in the office with other employees around. You walk up to the employee and say, "Bill, you need to do this by next Saturday. Don't screw it up." You then put the project on his desk and say, "Do you have any questions?"

This type of action is threatening and does not put Bill in a comfortable position. Bill cannot discuss his concerns or ask questions, even though you have superficially given him the opportunity to do so. The goal may not be clear to Bill and you have probably demotivated him.

Review the goal. During the introduction of a goal, review the goal with all employees involved. This occasion focuses on each employee's need to be fully aware of the goal's ramifications. During this review, the manager must be clear and discuss why the goal was set, who set it, and how it fits into the department and organization. Make the terms of measurement especially clear and unambiguous.

Imagine that you just introduced a goal to two employees, Susan and Lincoln. You would want to review the goal in the following manner: "Susan and Lincoln, let's review the goal for clarification purposes. You are to call these 500 customers, ask them about problems they've been having with Product X, and prepare a summary chart. You should complete this project in the next six weeks. We will review your progress every week, and you should complete the calling in four weeks. This survey is important to our company. The executive vice president of our department (customer service) has asked that we work on this. Your summary will be forwarded to quality control. The company needs to know what the most common problems are with Product X so that it can improve that aspect of the product. Do you have any questions?"

The delicacy of the goal-review process cannot be overemphasized. This is when the employees form initial impressions of the newly assigned goals. Much of the goal's future attainment (or failure) depends upon those impressions and the existing level of trust between the manager and the employees. Unfortunately, a low trust level between the individuals involved will surely sow the seeds of discontent and lead to eventual goal failure.

During goal review, the employees have the opportunity to fully express their opinions on the proposed goals. You must always listen carefully and avoid interruptions. While the principles of effective feedback apply here, the supervisor should be especially alert to neutral feedback, which may signal that a noncommittal attitude will surface. This type of situation should not be allowed to continue, because it could jeopardize the success of the goal-setting process.

Goal commitment. Since both the supervisor and employees have just finished working together in a mutual problem-solving situation, the employees will then formally accept the goal assignment. Granted, this is not always an "automatic" step, but it will probably happen, provided that the previous steps have been carried out. The supervisor and employees must mutually commit to the goal. All must truly believe that the goal is attainable and that both sides will give their full support. Once again, the trust level between the individuals will be an important factor. Finally, the employees must clearly see the benefits of goal attainment—both from an organizational and individual point of view.

There should be some type of goal commitment form that the supervisor and employees sign, which clearly states the goal itself, the time frame for accomplishing the goal, and the date the goal was set.

You might want to say to the employees, "Susan and Lincoln, now that we have discussed the project and its goals, we need to make sure that you feel comfortable with the project, what is expected of you, and the process that we will follow during this project. Do you feel that you can commit to the terms we have agreed upon?"

Retain flexibility in your overview. Recognize that difficulties may arise. Have a compassionate but firm attitude. Encourage and support wherever possible.

Following up. It is always the supervisor's responsibility to follow up with the employees on goal accomplishment through monitoring.

The truly effective supervisor plans thoroughly before taking the first step in the process. Whatever the supervisor's education, background, or experience, there is really no other way around the goal-setting structure. By any standard, the process is not an easy one: at the same time, however, it is one that remains absolutely vital to job fulfillment. Supervision of the delegation process, including the modification of goals, will be discussed in greater detail in Chapter 5.

SUMMARY

Goal-setting is the starting block of delegation. Without clear, measurable goals, delegations are sure to fail. By giving your delegatee realistic, challenging, and concrete goals, you set the framework for meaningful action plans and efforts directed toward a viable end. As we shall discover in the remainder of the book, you can use and refer to goals throughout the entire delegation process.

Conceiving well-defined, measurable, and realistic goals is a necessary part of a work plan, especially one that you are delegating to someone else. It would be difficult to describe a task to someone without indicating what you want them to accomplish, by what time, and in what way, and it would be unfair to expect them to guess what you might have in mind. It would, in fact, be impossible to assess their work, because the goals that would provide a yardstick for evaluation were not adequately considered.

You must develop goals before you can assign the work, then you must communicate the goals clearly to the delegatees. They are likely to have questions, or perhaps they may offer ideas about how the goals could be reached. Be prepared to answer questions and to listen and respond to comments or new ideas. Explain why the goals are important and how they help or contribute to the organization.

Let the delegatee know that you will be available for further discussion about the on-going progress toward the goals. Remember that the responsibility for achieving the goals is ultimately yours, but encourage the delegatee to feel a sense of increased responsibility as well.

CHAPTER 3 # COMMUNICATION:

*Barriers, Techniques, and
Continuing Feedback*

*Frown on lapses in information.
When people admit that they didn't
keep you informed, let them know you
don't want that kind of "protection."*

—Thomas L. Quick

C*hapter Focus:* This chapter will discuss how effective communication can improve the success of a delegation. Problems associated with communicating effectively and techniques for communicating more effectively are considered.

You need to think of communication as a two-way process. A good communicator exemplifies the idea that communication is a two-way process.

Communication is an integral and crucial element of the delegation process. Delegations often fail because of a breakdown in communication. Communication is the lifeblood of delegation—all the components of delegation require effective communication, from goal-setting to evaluation. Remembering our analogy of delegation as a relationship, we should put our effort into making communication part of our delegation procedure. The benefits of improving this skill for you and the organization include fewer complaints and misunderstandings, greater personal satisfaction for everyone, increased productivity and efficiency, and smoother working relationships and teamwork.

Communication involves a sender and a receiver exchanging and understanding information. It is important to remember that two individuals are involved. Both the sender and the receiver should actively participate. A good communicator exemplifies the idea that communication is a two-way process by practicing the following:

- clarifying the message
- listening to the message
- providing necessary information
- using appropriate language, tone, and volume
- requesting feedback
- exchanging ideas, feelings, and values
- using nonverbal signals to support messages

Clearly, the skilled communicator does more than simply relay a message. Communication involves not only the successful relaying of a message, but also the accurate reception of the message by the other party.

The problem, however, is that many barriers muddle the process and hinder clear communication. These barriers are numerous and, cumulatively, can create problems.

If you were to ask a computer programmer to write down all your appointments for the next year—all your meetings, vacations, days off, seminars to attend, association meetings to chair, and more— what might that person do?

The programmer might write it in a computer language or code, and if you were not literate in that language or code, you would not understand any of it.

That is not to say that you would not recognize all the symbols and numbers, but you would not understand the information. Although the message had been sent correctly, it wouldn't be received with the proper understanding. A communication problem would exist.

BARRIERS TO EFFECTIVE COMMUNICATION

Several factors obstruct effective, two-way communication. How many of these are you aware of when communicating with others? Think about how these factors can negatively impact upon the success of a delegation.

Differences between the communicators. This fundamental communication barrier between people stems from differences in backgrounds, personalities, beliefs, education, religion, life experience, and other areas.

Cognitive dissonance. Our ability to receive messages is limited by our tendency to hear only what we expect or want to hear. The human mind resists what it does not expect or want to perceive.

Judgmental inclinations. We have a natural tendency to judge or evaluate statements and to reach hasty conclusions. It is natural to evaluate a statement from your own frame of reference instead of understanding the speaker's point of view. This, however, does not add up to useful communication. Instead, two ideas are merely being advanced without an exchange of information.

Singular viewpoints. Our judgmental inclinations lead us to see situations from a single point of view, instead of considering a number of viewpoints. Operating with a closed mind prevents two-way communication.

Time constraints. Limits on time impedes in-depth communication. Many supervisors and managers, being busy people, tend to give hurried one-way instructions and then move quickly to the next task. The receiver can be confused or frustrated by such communication practices.

Fear of the consequences. People sometimes withhold negative information from others to protect a person's feelings or a friendship.

Defensiveness. Not only do individuals occasionally avoid giving information, but they often resist receiving it. When we are criticized, we often become emotional and excited. Defensive reactions to feedback on job performance are common.

Stereotyping. Stereotypes are attitudes favoring or rejecting certain groups without examining individual circumstances or traits. The need to understand numerous things forces the mind to arrange things into easily identifiable groups.

Absolutization. Absolutization is the tendency to see everything as black or white. This tendency distorts reality and oversimplifies situations.

Different vocabularies. Specialists have their own technical terms and jargon. The jargon is familiar to those within the specialized field but usually unintelligible to outsiders. Organizational meetings involving people from many specialized areas are often marked by incomprehensible jargon. For example, the increasing use of abbreviations and acronyms such as FRB and AMA (AMA can stand for American Marketing Association, American Medical Association, American Management Association, and more) can cause problems. It doesn't take many of these terms to turn a conversation into a soliloquy.

Different word meanings. Because many words have several meanings, word meanings can easily become confused in conversation. Words often convey meanings to a receiver quite different from the meaning intended by the sender.

Ignoring nonverbal signals (body language). The sender's nonverbal signals, such as tone of voice, gestures, and appearance, are the most important factors in determining how a message is received and understood. In general, senders are consciously attentive only to their spoken words. The senders are often preoccupied with choosing words and are unaware of the tone of voice (which may project a frenzied feeling), appearance (possibly inappropriate), or the irritation caused by their constant knuckle-cracking.

Distractions. While we are capable of performing several tasks simultaneously, we never do more than one thing at once perfectly, especially while engaged in listening. Employees should not do anything that might distract themselves or the speaker, such as answering the telephone or tapping a pencil, while listening.

Here are several reasons why we don't listen as well as we should:

- We allow the environment to distract us. (Don't you usually ask your secretary to hold your phone calls during meetings?)
- We have fallen into the habit of talking and interrupting too much.
- We are often thinking about many things. In these instances, it's not easy to fully absorb and participate in what is being said to us.
- We want to refute what the other person has said. We're afraid that if we do not do so immediately, we may forget to make that point or lose the opportunity to do so.

If you find your mind wandering while listening, make a conscious effort to focus on the conversation. Don't make the mistake of thinking that you can drop out of a conversation and catch up later on. Instead, employ good communication practices from the very beginning.

Do you recognize yourself engaged in any of these ineffective communication practices?

Employee: "Maybe we should think about other options as well."

You: "No, this is the right way to do it. The people in customer service can't criticize us. They could never understand our problems."

Employee: "When we talked about this yesterday, I don't think you told me when it was due."
You: "Yes, I did. Women just don't listen."

Employee: "The project is too much for me to handle. I have …"
You: "You have plenty of time. Just work harder."

Employee: "But …"
You: "Get working. You're wasting time."

ACHIEVING EFFECTIVE COMMUNICATION IN ORGANIZATIONS

Effective communication requires continual attention, as the barriers described above demonstrate. There is hope, however. The following techniques have helped organizations successfully establish open two-way communication.

Establish multiple communication channels. Creating more avenues for communication to occur will increase the likelihood of success. For example, you can set up a system for written communication. Supply a notebook in which staff members can write comments, a box for messages, or suggestion forms. Written systems provide another option for staff who are too busy or are too timid to communicate messages in person.

Encourage open communication. The supervisor should set an example of being open and honest. The more the supervisor provides feedback and ideas to employees, the more comfortable they will feel about sharing ideas and feelings.

To encourage open communication, the supervisor should reward rather than punish the open expression of feelings, opinions, or problems. A supervisor can reward openness by showing appreciation for employees who share negative or sensitive messages and thanking employees for their openness.

Consider expectations beforehand. Before delivering a message, a communicator should determine the expectations of the recipient. If the message is at odds with those expectations, the communicator must make the receiver realize that something unexpected will be coming. One way to do this is to force people to examine their own attitudes, stereotypes, and expectations at the beginning of discussions. Supervisors also benefit from analyzing their own expectations prior to every discussion.

Another way to break through expectations is to send an unmistakable signal that something different will be confronting the receiver. You can simply announce the unexpected message at the outset of the discussion. Or you can jolt people out of routines by changing the format, tone, or setting of conversations.

STRATEGIES FOR MORE EFFECTIVE COMMUNICATION

On a personal level, you can utilize many strategies to become a more effective communicator. Some of these strategies are detailed on the next two pages.

ACTIVE LISTENING: LISTENING AS COMMUNICATION

Listening is an active and complex process. We must train our minds to be perceptive and to accept information for discussion. Poor listening habits may result in conflicts, costly errors, and inefficiency. Proper listening will result in more accurate communication and more successful personal and professional relationships. Prosperous organizations expend time and money on interpersonal skills training, including communication skills that focus on listening.

Becoming an active and effective listener provides two important benefits. First, you may gain information from sources that you previously missed through poor listening. Second, even if you don't ultimately agree with the other individuals, at least they will feel that you are fair and open-minded.

If we are narrow-minded, then we cannot listen actively. Understanding the active listening process allows us to target our own problem areas and to develop active listening skills. Think of the process as an outline, and follow it step by step. When you deviate from the outline, refocus on it.

STEP 1. Listen

As the receiver, listen for the full meaning of the sender's message. Analyze body language, eye contact, and the verbal message to reach meaningful conclusions about the information.

STEP 2. Think

Form an initial opinion about the information. Even if you are uncomfortable with the information, continue listening carefully.

STEP 3. Respond

Reflect the message back to the sender. This clarifies the meaning of the message while compelling the participants to reiterate the message. If the reflected message does not satisfy the sender, it should be explained again in different terms. The process will continue until the sender is satisfied with the receiver's understanding of the message. Stay with a conversation until the message is clear.

STEP 4. Comprehend

The sender and receiver understand the message and discuss both points of view. Unfamiliarity with active

When you are the sender

1. Keep the conversation focused on its original purpose. This makes communication clearer and easier to follow for everyone involved.

2. Use "I" statements. "I" statements assertively express your thoughts and feelings. Instead of saying, "You make me mad," say "I feel ___." "I" statements defuse emotionally charged and hostile situations by showing empathy and a desire to share responsibility and control.

3. Ask questions and request feedback. Use open questions beginning with What, Who, When, Where, How, and Which. This shows interest, elicits more information, encourages the other person to talk, and clarifies the other person's interpretations.

4. Communicate your ideas at the proper time and place. The setting and each party's frame of mind greatly influence how well ideas will be received and exchanged.

5. Use nonverbal signals. This shows that you are interested in what is being said. For example, you can maintain eye contact, nod in approval, and lean forward.

6. Compliment the receiver. This enhances the receiver's self-confidence and encourages communication.

7. When you are upset, frustrated, or stressed, don't overcommunicate. Saying too much confuses the listener, drowns out your major points, and bores the listener.

8. Use the receiver's name whenever possible. This shows respect and acknowledgment.

When you are the receiver

1. Summarize by paraphrasing or restating, particularly with feelings. This shows that you are listening and are understanding what is being said, checks the listener's perceptions, and crystallizes a sender's comments.

2. Ask questions. Many of us are reluctant to ask questions when we aren't sure what the person means. This is usually due to fear of appearing stupid. A lot of confusion can be avoided, however, by simply asking someone to repeat or rephrase a statement.

3. Bounce feelings back to the sender. This shows empathy and clarifies the sender's position.

4. Respond to nonverbal cues. This clarifies the meaning of a bodily reaction, ensures that behaviors and words convey the same message, and shows understanding.

5. Give your undivided attention while communicating. Most of us can do well only one thing at a time. Activities such as whistling, shuffling papers, and looking away communicate a mood of indifference. Show the other person the interest and attention that you would have shown yourself.

6. Ask open questions. This obtains more information. Ask who, what, when, where, why, and how.

listening techniques by one party can obstruct communication.

You can develop listening skills by:

Disarming common listening barriers. Recognizing the barriers that repeatedly occur when you are listening can assist in planning to remove or overcome barriers.

Cultivating a listening attitude. Project an attitude of respect for the speaker and the message, and show that you are trying to understand and appreciate the speaker's point of view.

Drawing from several listening techniques. Employ specific receiving techniques to support a listening attitude.

Implementing active listening techniques allows supervisors to keep in touch with the opinions and problems of employees, thereby increasing morale, productivity, and professionalism. Being aware of the active listening process helps employees recognize and overcome communication barriers. Sometimes communication barriers can be overlooked or ignored. For example, an overburdened individual may not have time to listen to the needs and comments of others. A careful assessment of employees' communication techniques is the first step to overcoming communication barriers.

Developing good listening habits is one way to become a better communicator. Active listening will improve your interpersonal skills and can enhance your personal and professional life. So what are you waiting for? Get started on the road to better listening skills!

A manager in a small company relates how he improved his listening skills.

> *I used to be a horrible listener. I would look around while someone was talking to me, stretch, or put people off. I constantly drew conclusions about what was being said and assumed that I understood what was being said instead of verifying things with the*

other person. I really intimidated people, and people did not like talking to me.

I turned things around, though, with a lot of practice. Someone once pointed out to me some of the no-no's I was committing. I realized that I wouldn't appreciate it if others did those things to me while I was talking. I went to a seminar on listening and learned a lot of things about myself and about how to listen more actively and carefully. It's been six months since the first seminar, and I've gone to a total of four of them. Slowly but surely, I'm becoming a better listener. It's taken a lot of patience, practice, and thought. But the effort has paid off. My employees now are more willing to discuss concerns, ask questions, and give suggestions. I'm on better terms with many of my employees. Things get done a lot more easily and efficiently, now that I listen to what others are saying to me.

FEEDBACK: CONTINUING TO COMMUNICATE

Feedback, an essential component of communication, provides information about how you are perceived by others and how your behavior is affecting them. An effective communicator solicits feedback in order to check for understanding and to remove as many communication barriers as possible.

Giving and receiving critical feedback is the most difficult and threatening aspect of the communication process. Both receiving and giving feedback can cause problems. Receiving feedback can make a person feel uncomfortable, create cognitive dissonance, lower self-esteem, and create defensiveness. On the other hand, giving feedback can expose someone else's vulnerable spots, create feelings of discomfort in both parties, block communication by causing anger or defensiveness, and make the supervisor feel guilty or overly harsh.

People like to hear what is consistent with their own belief structures; they usually resist contrary ideas.

It takes an open mind to be able to listen to criticism. For feedback to be effective, it must be seen as an interaction in which both parties have needs that must be considered. Unfortunately, most people never learn feedback skills. We therefore give critical feedback as we receive it—poorly—and that makes us even more wary of feedback.

We will discuss later the importance of effectively giving feedback, as well as specific techniques for giving feedback during the delegation process.

SUMMARY

Communication consists of several parts, including sending and receiving a message, actively listening, giving feedback, paraphrasing, and asking questions. You may have to radically change your current communication style in order to use communication as a mechanism for achieving effective delegation. Practice and conscious effort will help you improve this delegation skill.

CHAPTER 4

MOTIVATIONAL TECHNIQUES THAT WORK:

The Dynamics and the Process

If you want someone to be for you, never let them feel they are dependent on you. Make them feel you are in some way dependent on them.

—General George C. Marshall

Chapter Focus: This chapter will help you turn your employees into more motivated, and thus more effective, workers. The role of motivation in delegation, theories about motivation, and how to motivate employees is discussed.

> *Employees are their own best sources of motivation. With patience and practice, you can help your employees become self-motivated to successfully complete delegations.*

Motivation plays an important role in the success or failure of delegation projects. Delegations can sometimes be boring or overly difficult, or seem irrelevant to an employee, and thus demotivate. Delegatees also may not be highly motivated to complete a delegation because it is not a regular part of their job. Correctly presented and designed, a delegation should motivate an employee.

Goal-setting, communication, and supervision form the foundation of motivation. Goals give targets for the delegatee to strive for and reasons to complete the project at hand. Communication is critical to motivation because it conveys the connection between delegation and the delegatee's self-interest, and can encourage the delegatee if done properly. Apply the techniques discussed in Chapter 5 to motivate your delegatees.

Benefits of effectively motivating your employees include higher morale, increased productivity, better performance, and employees' personal satisfaction.

Motivation cannot be instantly learned, because it is highly complex. Unlike a mathematical formula, the myriad factors involved in motivation are never black or white but shades of gray. Still, one can become reasonably proficient in the art of motivating others. While this skill is complex, the average supervisor, through a comprehensive understanding of motivation, can become an effective leader of others in the workplace.

THE DYNAMICS OF MOTIVATION

While several useful definitions of motivation exist, for our purposes we will define it as "an individual's desire to do something based upon a need." When a person is confronted with a need (either perceived or actual), the result is usually a motivation to perform specific actions for some sort of gratification. Once a particular need has been satisfied, the motivation to continue the actions diminishes and remains at zero level until the need arises again. Individual needs vary in many ways.

1. Some needs are short term, while others are long term.
2. Need levels vary greatly among individuals.
3. Need levels change over a person's life span.
4. Need satisfaction is a constantly changing, dynamic process.

Needs can be classified into three categories: (1) basic or survival needs, (2) safety or security needs, and (3) relationship or ego needs. We will examine these three categories to better understand the connection between needs and motivation.

Basic or survival needs. This category comprises basic needs such as air, water, food, and shelter. We tend to take these need-satisfactions for granted unless we lose them. For example, we all take breathing for granted, yet we would certainly panic if our air supply were cut off. Similarly, while the need for shelter is usually fulfilled for most people, it takes only a few moments of walking in a blinding snowstorm to experience the discomfort of being deprived of shelter.

Under normal circumstances, needs classified within the basic or survival category are usually well-satisfied for the average person. The desire for these short-lived needs, once satisfied, will diminish, only to return when the need resurfaces.

Safety or security needs. At a higher level are a cluster of needs related to our own safety and security, such as the need to be reasonably secure in our daily job. While the majority of needs in this category are common to all, it is interesting to note that their effect on individuals can vary widely. For example, a 45-year-old supervisor would be interested in the organization's retirement plan, while an 18-year-old new employee might perceive the year-end bonus as far more important. The key variable is how an individual *perceives* a given situation, not what someone else believes to be true.

Relationship or ego needs. It is widely accepted that needs of this kind are the most complex and are not as easily satisfied as either basic/survival or safety/security needs. In this broad area, we find the following kinds of relationship needs that fulfill our own ego requirements:

- need for a personal sense of importance
- need for belonging and acceptance from others
- need for achievement
- need to be loved and cared for
- sense of identity

While all of these needs can vary in intensity among individuals, we all seek need-fulfillment in these areas. The extent to which people *perceive* need-fulfillment in this category directly impacts upon their mental well-being and will ultimately have a corresponding impact upon job performance. Recognizing the perception factor can directly aid in the process of managing others.

Our need level within each category is heavily influenced by both external factors and our own perceptions. External stimuli are factors over which we have little or no control but that impact upon our lives in the workplace. At the same time, our perceptions of any situation may be influenced by external factors (for example, the supervisor at work), and hence should be thoroughly understood by all those who manage others in the work environment.

What Motivates People?

Based on studies in a wide variety of professions, organizational psychologists have reached a number of conclusions about what motivates workers. When the environmental factors are not adequately provided for (the pay is low or the environment is oppressive), workers become frustrated. Even when these factors are adequately provided for, however, there will usually be no significant positive effect, because these factors do not in themselves elevate an individual's desire to do a job well. Content-related factors, commonly referred to as motivators, are what do stimulate workers to perform well by providing a genuine sense of satisfaction. To truly motivate employees, a manager needs to focus attention on restructuring jobs so that employees can derive more satisfaction directly from their work.

But how does one go about restructuring an employee's job to take advantage of these motivating factors? Taking a cue from organizational psychologists, a manager should strive to meet the following criteria in delegating a task:

1. *Meaningfulness.* Employees must feel that their work is important, valuable, and worthwhile. If employees believe that their work is unimportant, it won't really matter to them whether or not they do it well. If employees believe that their work has a significant impact upon the rest of the company, they will work hard to see that the impact is positive.

As an example, imagine that you must develop an agenda for tomorrow's meeting, but you also need to make several phone calls for the reception afterwards. Time is running out, so you decide to delegate the phone calls to an employee. You pick Amanda, telling her, "I'm in a time crunch. I would like to write up the agenda for tomorrow's meeting. You could help by calling the caterers and janitorial department to confirm arrangements for the reception following the meeting."

Also consider the young factory worker, Sara, who was working to supplement the family income. The year was 1966, and Sara didn't think in terms of career as much as family. Sara had taken a job from 6:00 P.M. to 10:00 P.M. in a factory that manufactured jewelry, machine parts, and some metal pieces for a government contract.

Sara's job was to crimp one-inch brass tubes so they would close on one end. To execute this, she would take a tube out of the incomplete pile, place it in a groove on the machine, and pull the lever down slowly so that the tube would not be crushed. When she had exerted the right amount of pressure, she would return the lever to its beginning position, take the tube from the machine, and place it into the completed pile. Each tube took no more than fifteen seconds, so you can imagine how monotonous and boring this would be after a few hours.

Sara wasn't particularly enthusiastic about the job, nor was she complaining. She knew that she

*could do it for four hours a night and then go home
and not think about it until the next night at 6:00.*

*What does this have to do with motivation?
What could you say to Sara to make her want to do a
better job and work faster?*

*One evening as Sara was sitting hunched over
her machine, her supervisor approached and asked
her if she knew what she was making. Sara looked
increduously at him and gave a smart remark to
show her contempt that he would even think she
cared. But he persisted in asking Sara if she knew
what she was working on.*

*Sara admitted that she didn't. Her supervisor
then informed her that the little brass tubes were part
of a government contract, and were going to be part
of a lunar spaceship.*

*Now remember that this was 1966, three years
before the United States landed on the moon. This
was science fiction material to Sara. She reflected
upon John F. Kennedy's speech a few years before
and once again became caught up in the excitement
of the dream, and, although she still thought the
lunar landing was far-fetched, she felt the stirrings of
patriotism. Her reaction was one of competitiveness
in helping to be the first nation to put a man on the
moon. Sara no longer looked at her job as being
monotonous and boring. Her body straightened up,
her attitude changed, her productivity sky-rocketed,
and she couldn't wait to get to work each day.*

*The job didn't change. The environment didn't
change. The brass tubes, the machine, and the
method didn't change. All that changed was Sara's
perception of the reason she was doing her job.*

2. *Responsibility.* Employees must feel personally responsible and accountable for the results of their work. If
they simply carry out the plans and instructions of a
supervisor, they will derive little personal satisfaction

when things go well. If employees have control over the planning and implementation of daily tasks in their department, they will feel satisfied when the company is thriving due to their efforts.

Transfer responsibility, accountability, and authority as appropriate during delegations. Work with delegatees to establish goals and benchmarks, but leave action plans more to the delegatee. For example, you might say:

"Lisa, remember that this is your baby. You are not just doing this project for me. The project is your responsibility, and I will hold you to the guidelines that we agreed upon today. You make the decisions about how to do specific parts of the project, as we have discussed."

3. *Knowledge of results.* Employees must receive regular feedback on the results of their efforts. If they exert major effort on an activity but receive no indication as to whether or not it was successful, they will gain no satisfaction. Employees can only derive satisfaction from positive feedback.

Feedback clarifies expectations and goals. Employees can respond to feedback and adjust their performance. Giving feedback regularly can also head off a potential disaster by providing checkpoints. After the second week of a four-week project, you could say:

"Dave, you've been doing a good job so far. At this rate, you will complete the project successfully and on time."

4. *Self-interest.* All motivation is concerned with performance, meaning you are trying to get employees to perform more productively. Productive performance achieves job goals in the most efficient way.

Getting people to achieve their job goals productively isn't easy. Workers can't be expected to work hard and efficiently unless they see a benefit. Most people are motivated to achieve a goal only when they know it will help them satisfy their own needs.

Motivation depends on getting people to see the link between their job goals and their needs. Once they understand how the two are connected, they'll understand how they can expect to benefit from achieving the goals. And once they understand that hard, efficient work will produce a personal payoff, they will feel motivated to perform productively.

The best way for a delegation to motivate is to answer the question, "What's in it for me?" For example, a routine, mundane delegation might save an employee from having to work overtime later on, or to avoid working for a cranky, stressed manager. Or you might tell an employee:

> *"Although this job may not be glamorous, it is important. And for completing it, I will add to your Christmas bonus."*

Rethinking Motivation

Theoretical approaches such as Maslow's hierarchy of needs and Herzberg's two-factor theory force us to think about the most effective motivation techniques. Unfortunately, however, these theories promote faulty assumptions. First, previous theories assume that all employees are basically alike in their needs and aspirations. Second, past theories generally assume that all managerial situations are alike. The incorrect conclusion drawn from those two assumptions is that there is "one best way" to motivate employees that will always work.

Over the last ten years, much research has been conducted on motivation, and a new understanding of motivation, based on organizational psychology has emerged.

1. *Individuals determine their own behavior in organizations.* Although many factors influence the behavior of individuals, people basically make their own decisions about how hard to work, what level of performance to operate at, and how much loyalty to show.

2. *A combination of individual and environmental forces determines behavior.* An individual enters an organization with a unique history that influences particular desires and outlooks on the world. Different work environments may produce different behavior in similar people, and different people may behave the same way in similar environments.

3. *Needs and desires differ from individual to individual.* People tend to do those things they see as leading to desirable outcomes (rewards or goals), and avoid doing those things they see as leading to undesirable outcomes.

People are neither intrinsically motivated nor unmotivated. Rather, motivation depends upon the situation and its relationship to an individual's needs.

STARTING THE PROCESS

Since behavior is determined by both internal and environmental forces, managers need to examine both the person and the environment. Before employing specific motivational techniques, you need to do the following.

1. *Determine each employee's goals, needs, and desires.* You can find out this information by (1) simply asking employees about their goals and desires, (2) noting employee's reactions to different situations, or (3) formally collecting data through a survey.

Keep in mind that it is extremely difficult to change what people want, but relatively easy to find out what they want. The skilled supervisor focuses on discovering needs, not changing people.

2. *Determine desired performance and behavior targets.* Supervisors frequently talk about "good performance" without defining what good performance actually is. Motivating others requires determining the desired

level of performance and defining it in specific, quantifiable terms so that employees can understand what is expected of them.

3. *Make performance targets attainable.* Performance levels that lead to rewards must be reachable. If employees feel that the level of performance required to get a reward is higher than they can reasonably achieve, their motivation to perform well will be low.

4. *Link desired performances to employee goals.* If your employee values external rewards, the emphasis should be on promotion, pay, and approval. While rewards can be verbally linked to performance, an employee needs to see the reward process in operation.

If your employee values internal rewards (such as a sense of achievement), you should concentrate on changing the nature of the person's job, because that type of person is likely to respond positively to the increased responsibility, feedback, and challenge that inherently reward good job performance. Ask employees for their perceptions about the existing situation, because people's perceptions, not reality, determine their motivation. Many supervisors are misled because they rely on their own perceptions and forget to find out how their employees feel. Always try to focus on the employee's self-interest when delegating.

5. *Changes in outcomes should motivate.* Make sure that changes in outcomes or rewards are large enough to motivate significant improvement. Insignificant rewards will result in an insignificant effort and thus insignificant improvements in performance. Rewards must be large enough to motivate individuals to put forth the effort required to bring about significant changes in performance.

The importance of goal-setting can be clearly seen from this section. Using the principles of goal-setting to establish this foundation, you can now implement some or all of the following techniques for fostering motivation in your delegatee:

Encourage self-control. One principle of motivation is to shift control from the manager to the employee. Therefore, done properly, delegations should motivate. Employees should assume responsibility for planning and implementing daily activities to achieve the delegation's goals. Employees will work hard, not because they are being closely watched by their manager, but because they are personally committed to achieving the goals of the delegation.

Not all employees will be willing or able to function independently. Employees with low self-confidence can be assigned full responsibility for a limited project or for performing a specific function; both will support and develop self-esteem.

Promote staff development. A manager can motivate employees by providing employees with opportunities to improve their skills. The more skilled that employees are, the more likely they are to experience (and be rewarded for) success. The manager should help employees identify their specific training needs and secure additional training or resources. These resources may be in the form of reading material, in-house staff training sessions, or outside workshops and courses.

Link delegations to professional development when possible. Challenging delegations should motivate an employee if you clearly spell out that successfully completing the task could help the employee gain new skills or experience.

Encourage broader involvement. Most employees will feel better about themselves and more excited about their work if they are involved in their profession outside the department. If employees are involved in the overall management of their organization, they will have a stronger sense that their efforts are an integral part of a vital profession.

At the organizational level, employees' involvement can be broadened by keeping them continually informed on the status of the organization as a whole, by assigning them limited administrative responsibilities and involving them, when feasible, in major decisions.

Provide encouraging feedback. Give feedback to the delegatee as you monitor performance. Be specific when praising. Specific praise is more meaningful, credible, and personal than vague praise. For example, say "You are doing a good job handling customer complaints and returns," rather than "You are doing well." The first statement gives the employee something specific to think about and appreciate.

Also, as much as possible, encourage your employees when you give feedback. Encouragement communicates trust, respect, and belief in someone else. Discouragement results in lowered self-esteem and alienation from others. If you use any of these means of communication, you are a discouraging supervisor:

Constantly criticizing and pointing out mistakes.

Holding onto old attitudes ("You've always been like that") that can inhibit change or growth.

Having unrealistic expectations of others—specifically, that they should not make mistakes.

Instead, use encouraging words such as:

"What did you learn from your mistake?"

"You did a good job. . ."

"Keep trying even though you're frustrated. I'm sure you can solve the problem."

"You have improved. . . ."

"If you need help, you know where to find me."

Communication, then, is critically important to motivating delegatees. As stressed in Chapter 3, *how* you say something is as important as *what* you say. Encourage rather than discourage, and talk with the delegatee.

Remember: It is not easy to become an effective motivator. You will need to spend time and practice this skill. Over time, you will get a feel for what works with your employees.

You need to become adept at many managerial skills—goal-setting, communicating, and supervising—to become an effective motivator. This means you will need to review this chapter as well as others in this book. Be persistent. The rewards will be well worth it.

A FINAL PERSPECTIVE ON MOTIVATION

The difference between your best people and the others is you. A supervisor can turn some employees into top achievers, leave most in the average category, and keep the rest on the low end of the scale, all because of the supervisor's own expectations, unconsciously expressed by the behavior of the supervisor toward the employee.

It's what you *do* that influences employee performance. Telling an employee, "I have confidence in you" is useless unless your behavior shows you are sincere. You'll make progress by analyzing your behavior and becoming more aware of how you treat your employees.

The underlying message of this chapter is that employees are their own best source of motivation. If your employees' assignments are properly structured, they will be motivated by the results of their own labor rather than by external rewards and punishments. The manager's prime concern should be to help employees achieve control over and receive feedback about their work. Nonetheless, in motivating employees by concentrating attention on job content, the manager should not ignore the employees' basic needs.

CHAPTER 5

SUPERVISING A DELEGATION:

Preparation, Strategies, and Control

You do not lead by pointing and telling people some place to go. You lead by going to that place and making a case.

—Ken Kesey

Chapter Focus: This chapter will present the ways you can supervise a delegation and see it through to success. Strategies for managing delegations and special supervisory considerations are discussed.

Your good judgment is an important part of supervising delegations. If you're flexible and ready to modify your level of control when a delegation seems headed for failure, you can avert disaster.

Goal-setting, communication, and motivation are groundwork for delegation, but we should examine supervision to round out the aspects of implementation and follow-through. The basic principles of supervision apply to delegations as well:

- set clear goals
- communicate
- lead
- empathize
- motivate
- use positive reinforcement

Supervising delegations, however, requires techniques to deal with the special circumstances.

Delegations sometimes run into obstacles. For example, the employee may have difficulty completing the task, or may be resistant to it. On these occasions, the manager can step in and bolster the delegatee without taking the job back.

In this chapter, we will discuss techniques for supervising delegations, including preparing the way for a delegation, managing performance during a delegation, handling the question of control, and dealing with the psychology of employees.

PREPARING THE WAY

While the delegatee should plan and execute activities to complete the task, you can and should help the delegatee in several ways:

Review resources. Make sure there are adequate and appropriate supplies. For example, don't ask an employee to take pictures during the evening without supplying an appropriate camera.

Also, make sure that the resources needed to complete the delegation do in fact, exist. Wouldn't it be embarrassing to ask an employee to inventory your department's mail meters when you stopped using them a month ago?

Supply necessary information. Written information (such as detailed requirements) is sometimes needed for a task to be done properly. Reference material such as reports or blueprints should be provided if they are essential to the task. If these materials are not required, you can simply inform your employee where to find them in case they are needed.

Foresee difficulties. Your familiarity with a task can save time and trouble for your delegatee. You may not only be able to point out the complications you have encountered, but you may also be able to foresee problems that may arise because the task is unfamiliar to the delegatee. Passing along advice on how to handle difficulties will improve the chances of success.

Notify others about the delegation as necessary. If your associate is supposed to assist a project team, both the team leader and the team members should be given advance notice. Notify them not only out of courtesy, but also to facilitate the process, as work schedules may have to be adjusted or other plans made.

Loosen your grip. Something that you can do easily because of your skill and experience may pose problems for someone else. Try to guide the delegatee without taking over the job. Occasionally, there may be parts of a delegation that only you can do. Handle those, but leave the rest to the delegatee. For example, you may delegate financial research, but complete the statistical analysis and budget request yourself.

THREE PERFORMANCE MANAGEMENT STRATEGIES FOR DELEGATION

You can use three general strategies to supervise delegations so that they run smoothly.

STRATEGY ONE —Appraisal

Regular appraisal is a critical part of the delegation process. Several conditions regarding the appraisal process must be met for the performance management system to be a valuable experience to both the employee and the supervisor.

First and foremost, performance management must be practiced consistently. Following the performance management system only when convenient or when problems arise defeats its purpose.

For appraisal to be helpful, several points should be followed. Initially, performance standards must be clearly defined and communicated. Furthermore, supervisors must provide feedback daily to coach employees and give them concrete suggestions. Similarly, employees need to provide feedback to supervisors on how the delegation is progressing. You should address employee questions and concerns immediately.

STRATEGY TWO —Communication

In order for the performance management system to be effective, the supervisor must communicate with the delegatees. Follow the general techniques given in Chapter 3. In particular, you should ask them questions to foster employee self-exploration, encourage the delegatees to talk about their performance, and refer to specific observed behaviors and situations when describing problems or encouraging employees.

STRATEGY THREE —Coaching

People must feel valued and understood in order for coaching to be effective. If individuals do not feel valued or understood, they will not speak freely or try to improve, and will instead become defensive about their behavior.

Coaching can be defined as on-the-job training by which a manager teaches or helps employees improve their job-related skills and performance. By coaching employees, you can increase the probability of successful delegation.

Both the supervisor and the employee must help set the framework for fruitful coaching. The supervisor needs to empathize with the employee; cultivate a climate of trust and mutual respect; and acknowledge that the performance management system is a joint venture.

Likewise, the employee has certain responsibilities. These include: showing genuine interest in and concern for the job; helping set the climate of trust and mutual respect; and, like the supervisor, acknowledging that the performance management system is a joint collaboration.

Finally, both the supervisor and the employee must be willing to examine and discuss problems and feelings. A closed, domineering attitude on the part of the supervisor may temporarily bring the desired results, but it will not generate the changes in attitudes or behavior necessary for long-term improvement.

Now that both supervisor and employee understand the prerequisites for successful coaching, we can turn to the coaching process itself. Coaching involves five basic steps, although it may not be necessary to follow all of them. One or more of the conditions may be satisfied in some situations.

It can be helpful to use a sports analogy to think about coaching. For example, consider a situation in which you are coaching someone on tennis service.

1. *Explain why the skill being coached is important to the person learning it.* For example, point out that one's tennis service, which can be a powerful weapon, allows a player to win points outright and set up easy volleys. You may also establish a goal such as "hitting 70 percent of first-serve attempts" or "hitting my services with more spin and/or slice." Establishing goals will also motivate your employee by providing personally relevant targets.
2. *Explain how to do the job.* You might tell the tennis student to assume a certain stance, toss the ball in a particular way, follow through, and so on. Explaining a job will give the employee an idea of what to do and how to do it, thereby relieving anxiety and confusion.
3. *Demonstrate how to do the job.* You would now actually hit a service using the techniques you described or advocated. You may have to demonstrate a job more than once. Make sure to cover all the steps.

Sometimes it's easy to overlook steps when we have a lot of experience with the task.

4. *Give the employee an opportunity to practice the skill or procedure.* Let the person practice hitting serves. There is no substitute for practice. Practice makes perfect—or at least better.

5. *Give constructive feedback, pointing out the good and the bad.* You could compliment your student player on slicing the service well, or discuss improving follow-through. Encourage and communicate positively while also pointing out areas that could use improvement.

Practiced properly, an ongoing performance management system can promote a positive environment leading to greater individual, departmental, and organizational productivity.

What happens when you don't coach well:

You have given Jeff, your administrative assistant, a project to complete using a computer database, and you are coaching him on how to utilize a database. You show him how to create data cells and how to print out the information, and then you leave him alone to figure the rest out.

But you haven't shown Jeff how to correct errors or allowed him to try out the program with you there to help. He must now sit down and read a complicated, perhaps unclear manual, and use the time-consuming trial-and-error method to learn the database. He may continue using keystrokes that could be shortened if you had shown him how to do so.

Your experience would have saved Jeff time and frustration. Or you could have assigned a computer tutor to him. Either way, because you have not coached him well, Jeff does not know how to operate the database.

THE QUESTION OF CONTROL

Ultimate responsibility for a delegated task remains yours. Therefore, it is both logical and desirable for you to retain some control over a delegation.

Although some people believe that you either delegate or you don't, degrees of control are possible. In some situations it may be best to grant total independence and simply ask for results. In others it may be better for you to request occasional progress reports and notification of unanticipated developments. In still other instances, depending upon the employee and the task, you should exercise constant control, helping the employee develop self-confidence by giving more responsibility as it is earned.

When a delegation seems to be headed for failure, you can avert disaster if you're flexible and ready to modify your level of control. Much is at stake, including your employee's self-confidence and the project itself.

Making the Decision

Avoid launching a premature rescue operation when you see that problems may be developing. Making a delegatee deal with a tough situation or take a risk can be the best experience you can give.

You have to carefully decide how far to let a situation proceed before intervening. Consider the consequences. You have to weigh the impact of error or failure on different groups and individuals. How will failure affect your department, other departments, your suppliers, your customers, other associates, your delegatee, and yourself? Will reputation, confidence, morale, or cooperation be damaged?

Balance the benefits of the experience against the consequences of failure. Some of the best lessons come from a failed task, with the result being that people become more resilient and have higher expectations of themselves. If you conclude that the final result of a failed delegation is tolerable, stay your course, but minimize the damage.

Supervising by the Exception Principle

Frederick W. Taylor proposed the exception principle, which rests on the idea that you need only keep track of unexpected or unusual developments during a delegation. You need to know only significant alterations to established procedures or goals. Employees are expected to find the answers to their questions through established guidelines.

Four considerations should guide your use of this principle as you supervise a delegation.

1. Before implementing this principle, you should develop goals, policies, and procedures that delegatees can use to deal with minor deviations from planned performance.
2. Employees should seek answers on their own, except when there are no standard operating procedures applicable to a particular situation.
3. Although the activity should remain within certain general parameters, some deviation from planned performance should be expected.
4. Be prepared to adjust the guidelines and procedures as necessary. Alter the standards when they no longer effectively guide performance.

In order for the exception principle to work, you need a capable employee and a sound procedural and information base for the employee to draw upon. You will find that the time and energy saved are well worth the initial effort required to start using the exception principle.

Turning Around Reverse Delegation

Some delegatees take the easy way out and immediately seek your advice or want to bail out at the first sign of trouble. The employee may lack self-confidence, fear failure, or want reassurance from you. The delegatee often wants you to take the job back, in an attempt at *reverse delegation*.

Most of the time, you should usually hand the job back to the delegatee. It may seem easier to take over, but restrain that urge. Don't allow the employee to reverse delegate and make you rescind the delegation.

Take the job back only as a last resort and only when either (1) time constraints necessitate that you or someone else handle the task or (2) the delegation's failure will be too costly in the long run for various parties.

Three steps can help prevent reverse delegation and having to take back a job.

1. *Plan*. Identify the available resources, including time, skill, materials, and authority. Make sure that sufficient resources exist for the delegatee to complete the job. Overloading an employee, for example, will only cause frustration and make the delegatee more likely to try to reverse delegate a task.
2. *Communicate*. Announce expectations and evaluation criteria clearly, and provide constructive feedback so the delegatees can adjust their performance. Also spell out how you will or will not assist them. The delegatees will feel better about their position, and will work harder to reach clear goals.
3. *Train and/or coach*. Training programs can build self-confidence and willingness to take risks. Or perhaps you can coach employees to do task-oriented jobs. Either way, these techniques alleviate the employees' fears and make them more willing to tackle tasks.

Clearly, then, there is a step halfway between permitting delegatees to try to work out of the failing situation on their own and taking it over yourself. You can strengthen them and pass the delegation back by the following techniques:

- *Discuss the situation.* You and the delegatees should discuss the difficulties together. Help them understand what went wrong and why. Giving them all the answers may resolve the crisis, but will contribute little to growth and development.

    One approach is to guide the delegatees' analysis of the situation. Let them wrestle with the problem. Supply the information that will get them moving in the right direction.

    The discussion should focus on understanding the problem and examining possible solutions. Force the delegatees to ask questions to get them back on track. For example, they should think about the problem and its causes, possible solutions, the advantages and disadvantages of each, and other relevant considerations.

    You should reaffirm that you think they can make decisions, and that you *expect* them to make decisions.

- *Draw up a timetable and a plan of action.* Together with the delegatees, revise the timetable and action plan as necessary. Establish specific times for progress reports, and set intermediate targets to shoot for. These will often be revised versions of the originally established goals.

- *Give advice.* Point out a possible course of action instead of dictating complete instructions for them. Make it clear that the job is still theirs.

- *Provide assistance.* Recommend or secure the services of an experienced employee. For example, if the difficulty involves requesting new equipment or supplies, you can have the delegatees consult someone in the purchasing department or an employee with more experience in the matter.

- *Build confidence.* Make it clear that you're not replacing anyone and praise them for their work thus far.

- *Monitor progress.* Check on progress at regular intervals or at preestablished targets. This supports the employees and provides some responsibility.

- *Taking back and then returning delegations.* Sometimes you may need to take back parts of the delegation. Return them when the delegatee becomes more confident and performs tasks satisfactorily. Slowly and gradually increase responsibility.

Handling Reverse Delegation

An employee walks up to you and says, "I'm having trouble with the project you gave me. I don't think I can do it."

The employee has put you in a tough spot. Stand firm, though, and don't take back the job. You could say, "Let's talk about this before we make any hasty decisions. What do you think the problem is? How do you see the situation? How could we possibly solve it?" Listen to the employee's thoughts. After discussing the options, you might say, "I'm glad to see that you have ideas in mind about how to tackle the problem. See, you can approach this project if you put your mind to it. Let's set a time frame for implementing the necessary changes and talk about this some more."

Do not let the delegatee rescind responsibilities easily. Insist that the employee try again. You should not take back delegations unless failure to complete the job is too costly for the parties involved or unless time constraints mandate that you step in.

THE PSYCHOLOGY OF DELEGATEES

You must consider the psychological states of your delegatees. Anticipating their feelings helps you adjust your approach. The following are some of the reactions that potential delegatees may exhibit.

Resistance. You may occasionally encounter an employee who doesn't like delegations. These people generally have limited job goals and simply want to do their own work. Such a response is neither constructive nor cooperative. You can respond in two ways.

First, you can take back the delegation and give it to another employee who will be more willing to do the assignment.

Second, you can take the time to explain the delegation process and make it clear that the employee is not being taken advantage of. If you explain that delegation is commonly practiced, and if you can point to other tasks you have delegated with satisfactory results, your offer may be received more positively.

Bragging. Some employees may so desire the approval of their peers that they will exaggerate the significance of a delegation. They want to make a big deal of an assignment that you have given in a routine manner.

If you hear that delegatees are suggesting to others that they deserve a promotion or a raise, you should immediately clarify the situation. Decide in advance how you will handle the circumstance.

Grandiose visions. If both you and the delegatee view the delegation as a reward, then you will accomplish your purpose. But if the associate has ideas of great things to come, you may have to explain the situation. For example, say an employee mistakenly believes that a bonus will be awarded for completing a delegation. You could put the situation in proper perspective by saying, "I'm giving you the job so you can gain experience in dealing with customers."

SUMMARY

Supervising delegations requires planning, communication, monitoring, and coaching. Your judgment plays the most important role in supervising delegations.

Exercise your judgment carefully and wisely, yet decisively. Pay attention to this important aspect of delegation, and your delegation assignments are sure to be more successful.

Delegation provides an excellent way of giving your employees the chance to learn new skills and apply them in practice. You in turn will be able to focus on work you might otherwise not have adequate time for. Delegation can thus be seen as a mutually supportive process, which can enhance the sense of teamwork in an organization. Supervisors and delegatees will have the opportunity to see how the various jobs and tasks in the organization relate to one another, and most employees will appreciate the chance to expand the scope of their work and involvement with the company.

At the same time, delegation presents supervisors and employees alike with new challenges. If employees were restricted to only fulfilling the criteria in their job descriptions, the supervisor's function might be limited to simply doling out awards and dealing with shortfalls. The flexibility involved in situations where delegation is encouraged and explored, however, calls for greater creativity on the supervisor's part. Employees' abilities and readiness to learn must be taken into account; useful methods of assessment and feedback must be established; and the supervisor must be prepared to handle diplomatically any complications related to changes in the division of labor in the office.

CHAPTER 6

EVALUATING THE DELEGATION

Critical Areas in the Performance

*Look for the good things, not the
faults. It takes a good deal bigger-sized
brain to find out what is not wrong
with people and things, than to find
out what is wrong.*

—R.L. Sharpe

C*hapter Focus:* This chapter is geared toward helping
you improve the delegation process. The benefits of
evaluations to both you and the employee are discussed, along with conducting and following through
on evaluations.

*By underestimating the benefits of evaluations, many
managers are underutilizing a tool that can improve
employee performance. Evaluations should be seen as
exploratory sessions in which supervisors provide
support and resources to employees.*

An important, but often neglected, aspect of delegation is evaluating the process after the task has or has
not been successfully completed. The evaluation consists of more than just appraising the employee's performance. As the manager, you must also review your
own delegation practices.

Sometimes things go well, but delegatees are not
praised for their performance. Sometimes things go
badly, and they are not given constructive comments
and advice. Sometimes the supervisor should think about
possible improvements and examine the steps that were
taken in delegating and supervising the assignment, before blaming the delegatee.

Most supervisors and employees have negative feelings toward performance evaluations. This often results in shoddy, ineffective, or even nonexistent evaluations. By underestimating the benefits of evaluations, many managers are also underutilizing a tool that can improve employee performance.

Evaluations should not be seen merely as times to judge or criticize, or to be judged or criticized. Instead, evaluations should be seen as exploratory sessions in which supervisors provide support and resources to employees who want to improve their performance.

The evaluation period has the added effect of allowing supervisors and employees to come together and talk about past performance. It is a time when they can give feedback to each other, and consider how to improve future delegations.

WHY EVALUATE?

Managers often do not take full advantage of performance evaluations simply because they are unaware of the evaluation's overall role in management. It is important to understand *why* performance evaluations are necessary. Evaluations provide numerous benefits to employees and supervisors.

Employees Benefit from Evaluations

- *Evaluations give employees performance progress reports*. Evaluations examine how effectively the employee has carried out assigned responsibilities as measured against specific criteria. Furthermore, action plans for improving performance can be developed from evaluations. Overall, employees get an idea of how well they are carrying out delegation assignments.

- *Evaluations acknowledge employees* for their performance. Evaluations both motivate and give employees a sense of accomplishment when they achieve goals. As a result, employees approach delegations more enthusiastically.

- *Evaluations reinforce goals.* The evaluations should be based on previously set goals that specify (1) the delegation's goals and the individual's responsibilities and (2) the standards for measuring the employee's performance.

It is critical to link evaluations to established goals. Otherwise, the evaluations will become meaningless and threatening to the employee.

Evaluations are Beneficial to Supervisors

- *Evaluations give supervisors an idea* of the delegatee's ability and willingness to handle delegated assignments.

- *Evaluations give feedback to supervisors* about how they manage delegations. Perhaps a supervisor is giving unclear instructions, but would never know it if not for the evaluation.

- *Evaluations provide supervisors with an opportunity to establish good relationships* with employees. An open, two-way discussion in which ideas are shared should promote understanding and bring down some of the barriers that often exist between supervisors and employees. The supervisor can also show appreciation for the employee's diligence and positive attitude in completing the delegation.

The First Step: Preparation

Preparation is the first step to any successful performance evaluation. Both the supervisor and the employee must prepare. Each participant must be able to pinpoint specific instances—positive and negative—that reflect the employee's performance. Each should also plan to discuss specific accomplishments and how to build upon these in the future.

Evaluations should include each party's impressions of the worker's personal development and possible changes that may be needed to accomplish future delegation goals.

The supervisor should prepare using the following suggestions:

1. Review the delegation's goals and the performance criteria established.
2. Review conversations concerning the employee's progress and the feedback given.
3. Arrange a mutually agreeable time and place to have the evaluation discussion.
4. Make sure that the evaluation is held in a private place, and allow sufficient time for the meeting.

You can help employees prepare for the meeting by suggesting that they take the following steps:

- Review goals for the delegation.
- Review performance criteria and established targets.
- Review performance and compare to goals and performance criteria.
- Consider how your supervision has influenced the delegatee's performance, and how the employee could provide more guidance and assistance for you in the future.
- Think about changes in delegation procedures or interpersonal communications the employee may suggest to you.

Setting the Scene

The discussion should take place in the supervisor's work area, and the players should feel equal during the evaluation. Although most evaluations take place while seated at the supervisor's desk, many managers find it beneficial to sit facing the employee without a desk or barrier. This seating arrangement encourages a more relaxed atmosphere and creates open communication by both parties.

Getting the Point Across

At the beginning of the discussion, the supervisor should always define exactly what will be covered and in what manner. (Nothing is worse than a misunderstanding of intention in a performance evaluation situation.) Misunderstandings will only create problems in the relationship and may cause one or both parties to become distracted, which sometimes lead to a breakdown in the evaluation.

Aside from work performance, personal growth and development should always be discussed. It is important for the supervisor to listen for both the emotional and logical content of an employee's responses. Also, after each point the employee makes, the supervisor should summarize and give feedback. The evaluator should also clarify any questionable points. A supervisor's attempt to understand the speaker's feelings will tell the employee that the supervisor is really listening.

Starting the evaluation. You and the employee are seated in your office, and the evaluation is about to begin. You might start with these statements:

> *"The purpose of this evaluation is to review the delegation process and think about how you and I could work to make it run more smoothly. Please feel free to talk openly and discuss both your and my performance."*

> *"We will discuss your performance as related to the established goals, my performance in supervising and planning the delegation, possible improvements in the process, and how you think this delegation has contributed to your professional development."*

> *"On each topic, you will get to give your thoughts, I will provide my thoughts, and then we will discuss them."*

"As we proceed, let's make sure that we understand each other. So ask questions when you need to."

Listen and Learn

Active listening is the supervisor's primary role in an employee's self-evaluation. When the employee has completed a self-evaluation, the supervisor should respond in a constructive, positive manner by mentioning first the points of agreement, then the points of disagreement. During this discourse, it is important that you, as the supervisor, be supportive and nonjudgmental. Even if you disagree with a point the employee makes, you should try not to be overpowering. This would only cause defensiveness, which is to be avoided at all costs.

When discussing what is considered an employee's poor performance, the employee should be encouraged to work with you to solve the problem. Positioning such problem-solving in "we" or "our" frames of reference encourages the feeling that the supervisor is on the employee's side. For example, say, "We should work to make future delegations more successful," rather than "this is all your fault."

The quality of communication between a supervisor and employee has a greater influence on the effectiveness of the evaluation than any other factor.

To improve communication, you should (1) ask specific questions regarding performance, (2) stick to the topic, and (3) avoid blaming the delegatee. Combining these tips with those given in Chapter 3 will increase the quality of communication.

DEFINING PERFORMANCE PROBLEMS

Supervisors frequently have trouble defining a problem with an employee's performance. Such nebulous problems can include not working independently, a lack of enthusiasm, or repeated mistakes. How can a manager accomplish what needs to be done without having to direct such employees every step of the way? Why do some employees really care about their jobs while others do only what they are told (and then only if their supervisor stands over them)?

Any time an employee's goals do not match those that have been established, there is a performance problem. Before jumping to conclusions about poor performance, the supervisor must make sure of all the facts and be specific about the problem.

The more clearly a problem is defined, the easier it will be to find a solution. A desired performance statement might be: "To complete the research on the company's history by Friday." Not understanding what the supervisor considers to be "acceptable performance" is a common problem for employees. A statement like "John Snider has a bad attitude" does not contain specific information about actual or expected performance. A statement regarding actual performance might be: "John failed to research four out of six topics assigned." If you were John's supervisor you would know exactly what you need to talk to John about—the four topics he did not research.

Whose Fault Is It?

When faced with any performance problem, the supervisor must realize that there are only two possible causes—deficiencies in knowledge and deficiencies in execution.

- *Deficiencies in knowledge* are most easily identified. No matter how motivated employees are or how hard they try, they cannot do their jobs efficiently if they do not have the appropriate knowledge or training. A knowledge deficiency is the supervisor's problem, not the employee's problem. It is the manager's responsibility to make sure workers have the necessary knowledge and the demonstrated skills to do their jobs.

    Training is generally the solution to knowledge-deficiency problems. Training might consist of formal training programs, on-the-job training, or individual coaching and instruction by supervisors. Follow up after training to ensure that workers fully comprehend the skills and feel confident about their newly gained knowledge.

■ *Deficiencies in execution* arise when an employee possesses the skills and the knowledge to perform properly but for some reason does not. Unlike a deficiency in knowledge, a deficiency in execution often (but not always) is the employee's fault.

The following are four methods for solving execution deficiency problems. Make sure you try each one before you decide to take disciplinary action. They are linked to effective supervision as well as goal-setting, communication, and motivation.

1. *Set goals.* You know how to do this by now. Always clarify goals and expectations.
2. *Give feedback.* The supervisor needs to let employees know that a job done well makes a difference—to them, to their supervisor, and to the company.
3. *Remove obstacles.* The supervisor is responsible for making sure the workers have all the time and resources necessary to do the job. For example, if workers receive conflicting instructions, if they get higher priorities, or if poor working conditions interfere with carrying out their duties, they may be unable to do their work properly.
4. *Eliminate punishment.* Make sure the results of doing a good job are positive and rewarding rather than negative and punishing. Also, don't threaten employees with ominous consequences when trying to encourage performance.

A wise man once said, "People will behave just about as well as you expect them to." Sometimes when supervisors are aware of a noncooperative attitude, they begin to expect noncooperation. Guard against this attitude in yourself.

Expect cooperation! When you assume that people want to cooperate, they are more likely to do so. Succeeding in getting someone to cooperate is in the best interests of the teacher, and is just a matter of removing obstacles that block the path to success. Generating successful performance is the ultimate benefit of an employee review.

COMPONENTS OF AN EFFECTIVE EVALUATION

The following supervisory behaviors contribute to a successful evaluation meeting. Try to adhere to them as much as possible. The effective supervisor will:

1. *Give the employee time to prepare.* Employees like having advance notice of the evaluation session so that they can think about their performance. Give the employee an agenda of specific topics to be discussed as well as a self-evaluation form to fill out. The prepared employees may have any number of points to share about their performance or the supervisor's role in the delegation.

2. *Explain the purpose of the evaluation.* Clarify that the purpose of the session is to talk about the employee's performance on the delegation. Resist the urge to use the performance evaluation as a disciplinary tool.

3. *Separate evaluation meetings from problem-solving, coaching, or development.* One cannot act as judge and helper simultaneously. Separating evaluation meetings from improvement sessions gives the supervisor a chance to be both an effective appraiser and a good trainer and developer.

4. *Document assertions.* Facts and dates will make feedback more acceptable and meaningful to the employee. Similarly, you should stick to observed behavior and rely on first-hand evidence. Instead of saying "You do not seem very enthusiastic," say "I heard you say...," or "I saw you do... ."

5. *Ask for the employee's opinion.* Doing this establishes that the evaluation is a two-way process. The supervisor learns how the employee feels about various topics relating to delegation.

6. *Listen to the employee.* The supervisor must listen to the employee, just as the supervisor expects the employee to listen. This shows respect and establishes the joint nature of the evaluation.

7. *Accept the employee's feelings.* Accepting feelings of anger or displeasure is not the same as agreeing or believing the feelings are justified. Acknowledging feelings ("I see that you feel that way") and moving on prevents you from getting into a debate over the justifiability of feelings.

8. *Never criticize in an evaluation meeting.* Present information using objective descriptions, not evaluative adjectives. Don't say, "Your performance on project X is rotten" (or lousy, or poor). Instead, say "Your performance on project X is less than acceptable. Specifically... ." When performance is the reference rather than the person, it is much easier to accept problems and then do something about them. The amount of criticism in evaluation meetings has been shown to be inversely proportional to positive changes in performance.

9. *Provide specific feedback.* Statements such as "You're doing a good job" and "You'd better shape up" are almost without value unless accompanied by *specific* feedback on what the employee is to continue doing or to stop doing. If you say that the employee "shows initiative," talk about specific occasions on which the employee did indeed take the initiative.

10. *Pinpoint areas for improvement.* Jointly plan ways to improve performance. Focus on two or three performance areas, then concentrate on those areas during the next similar delegation.

11. *Ask for possible improvements in delegation supervision and management.* Have the delegatee answer

questions such as, "Did the delegator give me adequate, specific feedback?" "Did I receive clear instructions?" and "Did the delegator prepare the way or provide the necessary assistance and resources?" This step focuses on the supervisor's performance and gives the delegatee an opportunity to contribute to the evaluation and the delegation process as a whole.

12. *Allow sufficient time.* Take as long as you believe is necessary to discuss past, present, and future performance issues and to reach agreement on what will happen in the future.

13. *Conclude on an encouraging note.* Emphasize that you are now both working toward more successful delegations in the future.

SUMMARY

The ability to discuss performance with employees consists of planning and preparing for evaluations; communicating openly, honestly, and sincerely using "I" statements; and giving and receiving critical feedback. Although evaluations may seem like a nuisance or point of contention, they need not be so if approached and handled appropriately. Instead, well-conducted evaluations will help you not only with delegation, but also with more general performance issues.

As with other managerial skills, you will need to practice evaluating delegations, but your time and effort will be repaid many times over in future delegations.

CHAPTER 7 CONCLUSION

Whatever the source of the leader's ideas, he cannot inspire his people unless he expresses vivid goals which in some sense they want.

—David McClelland

As you have gathered by now, delegation is not a simple skill. While following the general guidelines outlined in this book may not guarantee successful delegations 100 percent of the time, doing so will help you become better than most other managers at delegating tasks.

As you begin to use the techniques presented in this book, keep in mind that effective delegation requires planning, persistence, and practice.

Planning. First, you must decide what is to be done and who is to do it. Then you must establish goals and link them to the employee's goals whenever possible. You also need to think about how you will communicate with the delegatee, prepare the way for the delegatee, and prepare for the evaluation meeting. Clearly, planning and preparation are crucial aspects of the delegation process from beginning to end.

Persistence. Delegation is a multitiered process requiring follow-through. Remember to constantly give feedback and communicate with the delegatee. When coaching a delegatee, you may have to demonstrate something more than once. Or when supervising, stay with a floundering delegatee. Don't take the job back immediately. Even when a delegation has gone well, follow through by conducting an evaluation meeting to round out the process. Overall, stick to your guns and follow the basic techniques presented.

Practice. Delegation is not easy to learn. You must develop judgment and people skills, both of which come only through practice. The specific steps you take will vary depending upon the situation and the individual delegatee. Be flexible enough to change your methods when that action is necessary. Review this book periodically to remind yourself of the important points of effective delegation.

Following these three simple principles of delegation will get you started you on the road to more effective delegation, which can free your time for the things *you* need to do. Delegation not only bolsters productivity, it also enhances job satisfaction, teamwork, and employees' skills. Effective delegation results in tasks being completed by the most appropriate person and in the most efficient manner possible. And that's just plain good management.

RECOMMENDED REFERENCES

BOOKS

Art and Skill of Delegation, Lawrence L. Steinmetz, Addison-Wesley, 1976.

Delegate: The Key to Successful Management, Harold Taylor, Beauford Books, 1984.

Delegation: The Power of Letting Go, Robert B. Nelson, Glenview, IL: Scott, Foresman, 1988.

Designing Complex Organizations, Jay Galbraith, Addison-Wesley, 1973.

How to Delegate: A Guide to Getting Things Done, Herbert M. Engel, Gulf Publishing Co., 1983.

Initiative and Managerial Power, Raymond F. Valentine, New York: AMACOM, 1973.

Leadership and Delegation, Bristol Poly, State Mutual Books, 1980.

No-Nonsense Delegation, Dale D. McConkey, New York: AMACOM, 1974.

SELECTED PERIODICAL ARTICLES

Baker, Guy E. "Keys to Increasing Your Productivity." In *Broker World* vol 11. (February 1991): 98–100, 138.

A task force interviewed a number of Million Dollar Round Table members to determine how they wrote more than 150 life insurance policies each year—a high rate of productivity. One common characteristic was delegation—each producer had a staff of helpers providing service and sales assistance.

Barratt, Alan. "Doing Business in a Different Culture: The Implications for Management Development." In *Journal of European Industrial Training (UK)* vol 13. (1989): 28–31.

The globalization of business means that many managers will increasingly operate in different cultures, and managerial skills that should be emphasized include delegation, which will enable the executive to save time and to train and motivate employees.

Buckland, Michael K. "Information Handling, Organizational Structure, and Power." In *Journal of the ASIS* vol 40. (September 1989): 329–333.

The delegation of decision-making and the effectiveness of information-handling are inversely related to one another.

Cadley, John. "Super Manager." In *Successful Meetings (Part 1)* vol 40. (May 1991): 63–66.

Although they have been trained to lead, to plan, to organize, to build, to perform, and to produce, executives may find that the training they have received in delegation makes them feel more like managers.

Callarman, William G. and William W. McCartney. "Reversing Reverse Delegation." In *Management Solutions* vol 33. (July 1988): 11–15.

The pattern of reverse delegation can be turned around by using training, resource planning, communication, and common-sense management.

Carter, Janet Houser. "When Work Needs to Be Assigned." In *Supervisory Management* vol 35. (April 1990): 8–9.

Knowing how to give effective assignments can be a powerful motivational tool, and will encourage employee creativity and commitment if done well, but it will destroy an employee's job enthusiasm if done incorrectly.

Cronan, Thomas E. "Early Warning Signals." In *Small Business Reports* vol 16. (September 1991): 53–62.

One of the first signs of an impending crisis is when a business owner becomes overextended, and the key to dealing with overextension is the delegation of responsibilities.

Cusato, Ray. "Empowering Salespeople to Boost Sales." In *Small Business Reports* vol 16. (March 1991): 26–31.

The role of the sales manager is to create a self-motivated and self-managing salesforce; to accomplish this, sales managers must recognize the potency of empowerment.

Davidson, Jeffrey P. and Anthony Alessandra. "Motivating Your Staff." In *Texas Banking* vol 76. (November 1987): 30–31.

A good supervisor must know how to motivate staff. The delegation of tasks to those employees who show enthusiasm and initiative can be helpful in motivating people, and it also reduces the supervisor's workload.

Feuer, Dale. "How Women Manage." In *Training* vol 25. (August 1988): 23–31.

Twenty years after women flooded the workplace, the questions concerning why female managers are overrepresented in low-level, low-status positions still are being asked. Instead of delegating work to make time for more important tasks, many female managers chase after their subordinates, finishing their work and cleaning up after them.

Fritz, Roger. "How Do You Rate as a Manager?" In *Management Solutions* vol 33. (February 1988): 28–32.

Delegation is one of the five areas of managerial proficiency.

Hurley, Mike. "Be a Businessman or Get Buried." In *National Underwriter (Life/Health/Financial Services)* vol 94. (July 3, 1990): 11, 32.

If goals are not set, they cannot be met. Delegation, standardization, and mechanization are important elements of both time and of management.

Kanter, Rosabeth Moss and Barry A. Stein. "Unloading Overload." In *Management Review* vol 76. (November 1987): 22, 24.

Extreme forms of overload can be eliminated if the manager utilizes an improved system design that includes the delegation of both authority and responsibility.

Kirby, Tess. "Delegating: How to Let Go and Keep Control." In *Working Woman* vol 15. (February 1990): 32, 37.

To delegate effectively, managers must strike a balance between letting go of a project and guiding it toward completion.

Knippen, Jay T. and Thad B. Green. "Delegation." In *Supervision* vol 51. (March 1990): 7–9, 17.

Effectively done, the benefits of delegation offer many positive rewards. On the other hand, if delegation is ineffective, the outcome can be disastrous to the organization.

Lawrie, John. "Turning Around Attitudes About Delegation." In *Supervisory Management* vol 35. (December 1990): 1–2.

Although there are good reasons for delegating in the workplace, evidence suggests that delegation does not occur as frequently, or with the sustained intensity, that it should.

Longenecker, Clinton O. "The Delegation Dilemma." In *Supervision* vol 52. (February 1991): 3–5.

Employee complaints about lack of feedback or lack of authority suggest that the process of delegation is not being fully practiced by their superiors.

McConnell, Charles R. "A New Look at Delegation: The Supervisor's Personal Approach." In *Health Care Supervisor* vol 5. (April 1987): 77–89.

Effective delegation is an important management tool, but it is often overlooked and generally misunderstood.

Nelson, Robert B. "Mastering Delegation." In *Executive Excellence* vol 7. (January 1990): 13–14.

One key measure of a manager's effectiveness lies in the ability to get things done through other people. By delegating, others do much of the work, giving the executive more time to manage, plan, and take on larger jobs.

Perry, Phillip M. "Techniques for Time & Priority Management." In *Legal Assistant Today* vol 8. (July/August 1991): 36–44.

Law firms are beginning to implement effective techniques to make their legal assistants more effective workers. Tasks that do not require the expertise of a paralegal should be delegated to clerks or secretaries.

Posner, Bruce G. "Looking Out for Number 2." In *Inc.* vol 13. (July 1991): 42–46.

Entrepreneurs need to learn how to delegate and work closely and productively with a second-in-command person.

Raudsepp, Eugene. "How to Delegate Effectively." In *Machine Design* vol 61. (April 20, 1989): 117–120.

Managers who practice the art of delegating properly will always accomplish more than those who refuse to let go of projects.

Schwartz, Andrew E. "The Why, What, and to Whom of Delegation." In *Management Solutions* vol 32. (June 1987): 31–38.

By learning to effectively delegate, managers can free themselves from routine and repetitive functions, ensure that the work is done by the right person, and increase the motivation, confidence, and personal and professional growth of subordinates.

Sherriton-Barnett, Jacalyn. "Developing a High Performance Staff." In *Rural Telecommunications* vol 7. (Spring 1988): 22–23.

The development of a high-performance staff involves delegating responsibility, developing communication systems that provide employees with relevant information, and coaching employees on how to perform new assignments.

Stern, David. "Getting the Most Out of Your Day." In *Business Credit* vol 91. (July/August 1989): 48–51.

Effective delegation not only saves hundreds of hours of unnecessary work, but it also provides invaluable training for subordinates.

INDEX

TITLES THAT GENERATE SUCCESS!

Business Success Series

Seasoned professionals offer common sense advice and facts on how to master job techniques that will generate success. Also included are interesting and informative case histories and insightful quotes. Each book: Paperback, $4.95, Can. $6.50, 96 pp., 4 3/16" x 7"

Conduct Better Job Interviews Wilson (4580-7)
Delegating Authority Schwartz (4958-6)
How To Negotiate a Bigger Raise Hartman (4604-8)
Making Presentations With Confidence Buchan (4588-2)
Maximizing Your Memory Power Lapp (4799-0)
Motivating People Smith (4673-0)
Running a Meeting That Works Miller (4640-4)
Time Management Hochheiser (4792-3)
Using the Telephone More Effectively Bodin (4672-2)
Winning With Difficult People Bell & Smith (4583-1)
Writing Effective Letters and Memos Bell (4674-9)

Prices subject to change without notice. Books may be purchased at your bookstore or by mail from Barron's. Enclose check or money order for total amount plus sales tax where applicable and 10% for postage and handling (minimum charge of $1.75, Canada $2.00). ISBN PREFIX: 0-8120

Barron's Educational Series, Inc.
250 Wireless Blvd., Hauppauge, NY 11788
In Canada: Georgetown Book Warehouse
34 Armstrong Ave., Georgetown, Ont. L7G 4R9